THE ENGLISH
GRADUAL

PART II — THE PROPER

THE ENGLISH GRADUAL

PART II
THE PROPER FOR THE LITURGICAL YEAR

Edited by

FRANCIS BURGESS

Musical Director of the Gregorian Association

THE PLAINCHANT PUBLICATIONS COMMITTEE

50 WOODVILLE ROAD, LONDON, N.W.11

These simple settings of the Introits, Graduals, Alleluias, Tracts, Offertories and Communions are intended for the use of parish choirs at the principal Service on Sundays and Holy-days throughout the Christian year. It is now more than forty years since the *Altar Hymnal* was issued, with the texts of the Proper and suggestions for chanting them. Since that time several selections from those texts have been published with the English words adapted to their Plainchant melodies in one form or another. But the progress of liturgical education has carried us beyond the selective stage. The merit of the present work lies in the provision of a simple method of singing the Proper on all Sundays and on certain other days, without displacing altogether the popular hymns which have attained a position of almost too great a prominence in the scheme of English worship.

The texts adopted (and the numbering of them) are those contained in the *English Hymnal*. The inclusion of the Proper is not the least of the many valuable features of that book, the proprietors of which have generously permitted their arrangement to be followed in the present work. In every case where the text of the Western Rite differs from that of the *English Hymnal* it is included as an alternative, printed in italics.

The forms of the Tones used throughout for the Introits, Graduals, Offertories and Communions are those associated by tradition with the Eucharist rather than with the Office. They represent the Tones in what is perhaps their oldest shape. Certain of their features, such as their double intonations and the slight elaboration of their cadences, give them a character which is distinct from that of the Tones customarily associated with the recitation of the Psalter. They have been used experimentally for their present purpose in a number of places during the past five years, and experience has shown that it is advisable to note out each text in full, a plan which has greatly enlarged the original scheme for this volume.

The following practical notes may be found of use to choirs:-

The *Introit* is begun as soon as the Celebrant approaches the altar. In those churches which follow the Sarum customs the Introit is repeated after the psalm-verse as well as after *world without end. Amen.* Elsewhere the Introit is repeated only once, as shown in the body of the book. In Passiontide, *Glory be* is omitted.

The *Gradual* is begun as soon as the Epistle is ended.

The *Alleluia* or *Tract* follows immediately upon the Gradual. It is neither necessary nor desirable for the organist to modulate from the last note of the Gradual to the first note of the piece which follows. A momentary pause will be needed, but nothing more.

During Easter-tide (though not on Easter-Day)
the Gradual is superseded by an Alleluia which
precedes, but does not displace, the Alleluia
which normally would follow. The two Alleluias, therefore, with their verses, are sung in
succession. This need present no difficulty, as
the result is exactly set out on pages 73 and 74
and on every subsequent occasion to which it
applies.

The *Sequence*, when it occurs, should be begun
immediately the Alleluia-verse is finished and
before the Alleluia itself is repeated for the last
time. This final Alleluia is not sung until the
end of the Sequence has been reached, and then
only to a brief musical phrase in the tonality of
the Sequence-melody. It has been found necessary, for the sake of clearness, to include the
Sequences on those days when they are of obli-
gation, and if the arrangement shewn on pages
70 and 72 and elsewhere be followed strictly no
practical difficulty need arise. Those churches
which follow the Sarum customs will omit the
Amen given at the end of each Sequence and pro-
ceed directly to the final *Alleluia*.

The *Offertory* is begun as soon as the Celebrant
begins to recite the Offertory at the altar.

The *Communion* is begun immediately after the
conclusion of the *Agnus Dei*.

Organ harmonies to all the Tones used in this book may be obtained from the publishers. Accompaniments to the Sequences will be found in the *En-lish Hymnal*.

The texts are arranged for antiphonal singing between Cantors and Choir, with certain passages (marked *Full*) for Cantors and Choir to sing together. The number of Cantors should vary according to the dignity of the occasion. On Solemn Feasts, four Cantors should be employed, if so many may be had. On Double and Semi-double Feasts and on ordinary Sundays the Cantors should be two in number. On Simple Feasts and Ferias only one Cantor is permitted.

It is very desirable that choirs using the settings of the Proper which this volume contains should make every effort to supplement these simple inflexions by learning the authentic Plainsong melodies to as many of the texts as possible. To this end the Editor desires to draw attention to the collection of Introits for Sundays and Festivals, edited by the late Dr. Palmer, and published at St. Mary's Convent, Wantage. To that book may be added the collection of Graduals, Alleluias and Tracts, obtainable from the same source.

F. B.

657   ADVENT SUNDAY

Introit   Tone VII

Cantors

Un - to thée, O Lórd, lift I úp my sóul; O my Gód,

in thée have I trústed, let me nót be con - fóund - ed:

Choir

néi - ther let mine énemies tríumph over me; for áll théy

FINE

that lóok for thee shall nót be a - shám - ed.

Cantors   *Choir*

Ps. Shéw me thy ways, O Lórd: and téach me thy páths.

Cantors

Gló - ry be to the Fáther, and to the Són, and to the

Choir

Hó-ly Ghóst. As it wás in the begínning, is nów, and

Full

éver sháll be: wórld withóut énd. Amen. Un - to thée (*etc.*)

Gradual   Tone V

Cantors   *Choir*

For all théy that lóok for thée: shall nót be ashámed, O Lórd.

Cantors   *Choir*

℣. Make knówn to mé thy wáys, O Lórd: and teách me thý paths.

ADVENT SUNDAY (continued)

Alleluia   Tone VI

Al - le - lú - ia.   Al - le - lú - ia.

℣. Shéw us thy mér - cy, O Lórd: and gránt us thý

sal - vá - tion.   Al - le - lú - ia.

Offertory   Tone II

Un - to thée, O Lórd, líft I úp my sóul; O my Gód,

in thée have I trústed, let me nót be con - fóund - ed

néi - ther let mine énemies tríumph over me;

for áll théy that lóok for thee shall nót be a - shámed.

Communion   Tone I

The Lórd shall shéw lov - ing_ kínd - ness:

and our lánd shall gíve her ín - crease.

658   ADVENT II

Introit   Tone VII

Cantors

O péo - ple of Síon, behóld, the Lórd is nígh at hánd

Choir

to re-déem the ná - tions: and in the gládness of your

héart the Lórd shall cáuse his gló-ri - ous vóice to

FINE   *Cantors*

be héard. *Ps.* Héar, O thou Shépherd of Is - ra - el:

Choir   *Cantors*

thou that léadest Jóseph like a shéep. Gló-ry be . . . .

Choir

and to the Hó-ly Ghóst. As it wás.. and éver sháll be:

Full

wórld with-óut énd. A - men. O péo - ple (*etc.*)

Gradual   Tone V

Cantors   *Choir*

Out of Síon hath Gód appéared: in pérfect béauty.

Cantors   *Choir*

℣. Gáther my sáints to-géther ún-to me: thóse that have

máde a cóvenant with mé with sác - ri - fíce.

ADVENT II (continued)

Alleluia   Tone VI

Cantors   *Choir*

Al - le - lú - ia.   Al - le - lú - ia.

Cantors

℣. For the pówers of héaven shall be shá - ken:
℣. *I was glád when they sáid un - to mé:*

Choir

and théy shall sée the Són of mán cóming in a clóud with pówer
we will gó into the

Full

and great glö - ry.   Al - le - lú - ia.
hoúse of the Lórd.

Offertory   Tone II

Cantors

Wílt not thou túrn agáin, O Gód, and quícken us;

Choir

that thy péo - ple may re - jóice in thee: shéw us

thy mércy, O Lórd; and gránt us thy sal - vá - tion.

Communion   Tone I

Cantors

Je - rú - salem, háste thee, and stánd on hígh:

Choir

and be - hóld the jóy and gládness that cómeth

unto thee from Gód thy Sá - viour.

659　　　　Advent III

Introit　　　　　　　　　　　　　　Tone VII

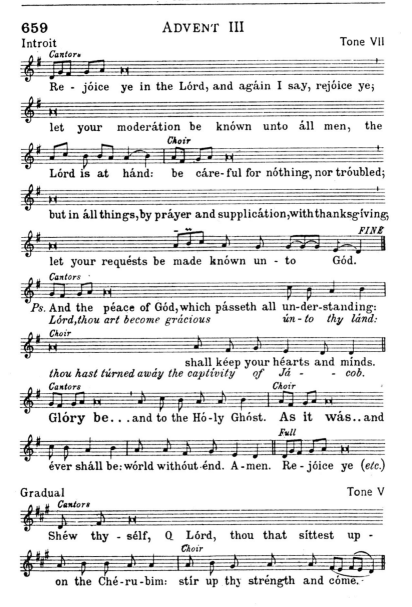

Re - jóice ye in the Lórd, and agáin I say, rejóice ye;

let your moderátion be knówn unto áll men, the

Lórd is at hánd: be cáre-ful for nóthing, nor tróubled;

but in áll things,by práyer and supplicátion,with thanksgíving;

FINE

let your requésts be made knówn un - to Gód.

Ps. And the péace of Gód,which pásseth all un-der-standing:
Lórd,thou art become grácious　　　　　ún - to　thy lánd:

shall kéep your héarts and mínds.
thou hast túrned awáy the captívity　of　Já - - cob.

Glóry be... and to the Hó-ly Ghóst. As it wás.. and

Full

éver sháll be: wórld withóut énd. A - men. Re - jóice ye (*etc.*)

Gradual　　　　　　　　　　　　　　Tone V

Shéw thy - sélf, Q Lórd, thou that síttest up -

on the Ché-ru-bim: stír up thy stréngth and cóme.

ADVENT III (continued)

Cantors

℣. Héar, O thou Shép - herd of Is - ra - el:

Choir

thou that léad-est Jó - seph like a sheep.

Alleluia   Tone VI

Cantors   *Choir*

Al - le - lú - ia. Al - le - lú - ia.

Cantors   *Choir*

℣. Stír up thy stréngth, O Lórd: and cóme and hélp us.

Full

Al - le - lú - ia.

Offertory   Tone II

Cantors

O Lórd, thou art become grácious unto thy lánd;

thou hast túrned awáy the cap-tí-vi - ty of Já - cob:

Choir

thou hast forgíven the of-fénce of thy péo - ple.

Communion   Tone I

Cantors

Sáy to thém that are of a féar - ful héart:

Choir

Be stróng, féar not; behóld, your Gód will cóme and sáve you.

660   ADVENT IV

Introit   Tone VII

Cantors

Re - mém - ber us, O Lórd, with the fávour
Drop dówn, ye héavens, from abóve,

that thou béarest unto thy péople; O vísit us with
and lét the skíes pour

Choir

thy sal - vá - tion: that wé, behólding the felícity
down rígh-teous-ness: let the éarth ópen,

of thy chósen, may rejóice in the gládness of thy péople;

FINE

and may glóry with thine in - hé - ri - tance.
and bring fórth a Sá - viour.

Cantors

Ps. We have sín - ned with our fá - thers:
Ps. The héa - vens decláre the gló - ry of Gód:

Choir

we have dóne a - míss and dealt wíck - ed - ly.
and the fírmament shéw - eth his hán - di - work.

Cantors

Gló - ry be . . . . . . and to the Hó - ly Ghóst.

Choir

As - it wás . . . . and év - er sháll be:

Full

wórld with-óut énd. A - men.   Re - mém-ber us *(etc.)*
                                     Drop dówn, ye héavens (etc.)

ADVENT IV (continued)

Gradual   Tone V

Cantors

The Lórd is nígh unto áll them that cáll up - on him:

Choir

yéa, all súch as cáll up - on him fáith - ful - ly.

Cantors

℣. My móuth shall spéak the práise of the Lórd:

Choir

and let áll flesh give thánks un-to his hó-ly Name.

Alleluia   Tone VI

Cantors   Choir

Al - le - lú - ia.   Al - le - lú - ia.

Choir   Choir

℣. Cóme, O Lórd, and tár-ry not: forgíve the misdéeds

Full

of thy péo - ple.   Al - le - lú - ia.

Offertory   Tone II

Cantors

Be stróng, féar not;   behóld, our Gód will
Hail, Má - ry, full of gráce;

Choir

cóme with a ré - com-pense: blést art thóu among
the Lórd is with thee: bléss-ed art thóu among

he will cóme, and sáve us.
wómen, and bléssed is the frúit of thy wómb.

Communion   Tone I

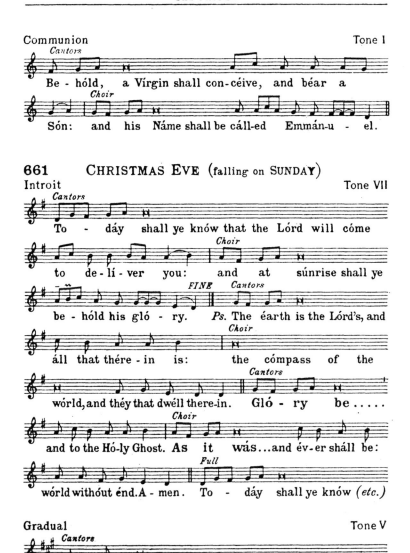

Cantors

Be - hóld, a Vírgin shall con-céive, and béar a

Choir

Són: and his Náme shall be cáll-ed Emmán-u - el.

661   CHRISTMAS EVE (falling on SUNDAY)

Introit   Tone VII

Cantors

To - dáy shall ye knów that the Lórd will cóme

Choir

to de-lí-ver you: and at súnrise shall ye

FINE *Cantors*

be - hóld his gló - ry. *Ps.* The éarth is the Lórd's, and

Choir

áll that thére-in is: the cómpass of the

Cantors

wórld, and théy that dwéll there-in. Gló - ry be . . . . .

Choir

and to the Hó-ly Ghost. As it wás...and év-er sháll be:

Full

wórld without énd. A - men. To - dáy shall ye knów *(etc.)*

Gradual   Tone V

Cantors

To - dáy shall ye knów that the Lord will

CHRISTMAS EVE (continued)

cóme to de - lí - ver you: and at súnrise shall ye be -

Cantors

hóld his gló - ry.   ℣. Héar, O thou Shépherd of

Israel; thóu that léadest Jó - seph like a sheep:

Choir

shéw thyself álso, thóu that síttest upón the Chérubim;

before Ephraim, Bénjamin, and Ma - nás - ses.

Alleluia   **Tone VI**

Cantors   *Choir*

Al - le - lú - ia. Al - le - lú - ia.

Cantors

℣. On the mórrow the iníquity of the éarth shall be

Choir

blót - ted óut: and the Sáviour of the wórld shall

Full

réign ó - ver us. Al - le - lú - ia.

Offertory   **Tone II**

Cantors

Líft up your héads, O ye gátes; and bé ye

lift úp, ye   év - - er - lást - ing doors:

Choir

and   the   Kíng of gló - ry   shall cóme in.

Communion   Tone I

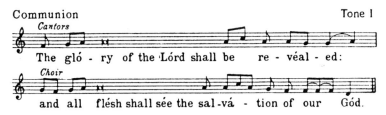

Cantors

The gló - ry of the ·Lórd shall be   re - véal - ed:

Choir

and all flésh shall sée the sal -vá - tion of our   Gód.

662   CHRISTMAS (at MIDNIGHT)

Introit   Tone VII

Cantors   *Choir*

The   Lórd hath sáid un - to   me: Thóu art my Són,

FINE *Cantors*

this dáy have I   be-gót - ten ·   thee. *Ps.* Whý do

Choir

the héathen so fúriously ráge to-gé - ther: and whý do

Cantors

the péople i - má-gine a váin thing? Gló - ry   be...

Choir

and to the Hó - ly Ghóst. As   it   wás... and év- er

Full

sháll be: wórld withóut énd. A - men. The   Lórd hath *(etc.)*

CHRISTMAS at MIDNIGHT (continued)

Gradual

Cantors

In the day of thy power shall the people offer thee

Choir

free-will offerings with an hó - ly wór - ship: the

dew of thy birth is of the womb of the morn-ing.

Cantors   *Choir*

℣. The Lórd said ún - to my Lord: Sít thou on my ríght hánd;

until I máke thine é - ne-mies thy fóot - stool.

Alleluia   Tone VI

Cantors   *Choir*

Al - le - lú - ia. Al - le - lú - ia.

Cantos   *Choir*

℣. The Lórd said ún - to me: Thóu art my Són; this dáy

Full

have I be-gót-ten thee. Al - le - lú - ia.

Offertory   Tone II

Cantors

Let   the   héa - vens re-jóice, and   let   the   éarth

Choir

be glád: be-fóre the Lórd, for   hé   is   cóme.

Communion   Tone I

Cantors   *Choir*

The déw of   thy bírth: is   of the wómb of the mórn-ing.

662ᴬ CHRISTMAS (at DAYBREAK)

Introit Tone VII

Cantors

Light shall shíne todáy upon us; for unto ús the

Choir

Lórd is bórn: and his Náme shall be cálled Wónderful,

Míghty Gód, the Prínce of péace, Fáther of the wórld to

FINE

cóme; of whose kíngdom there shall be nó end.

Cantors

Ps. The Lórd is Kíng and hath pút on glórious ap-pá-rel:

Choir

the Lórd hath pút on his appárel, and gírded himsélf with stréngth.

Cantors *Choir*

Gló-ry be... and to the Hó-ly Ghóst. As it wás... and

Full

év-er sháll be: wórld withóut énd. A-men. Líght shall shíne *(etc.)*

Gradual Tone V

Cantors

Bléss-ed is hé that cómeth in the Náme of the Lórd:

Choir *Cantors*

Gód is the Lórd, who hath shéw-ed us líght. ℣. Thís is

Choir

the Lórd's dó-ing: and it is már-vellous in óur eyes.

CHRISTMAS at DAYBREAK (continued)

Alleluia   Tone VI

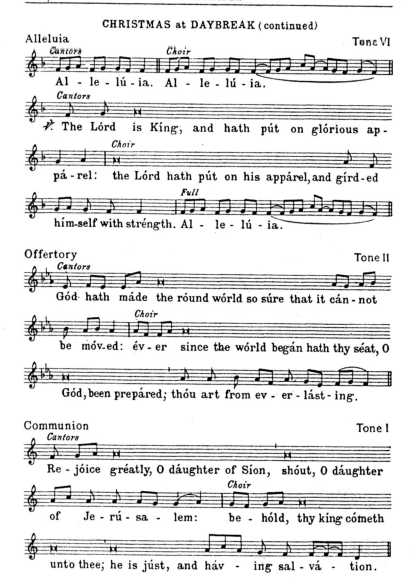

Al - le - lú - ia. Al - le - lú - ia.

℣. The Lórd is Kíng, and hath pút on glórious ap-

pá - rel: the Lórd hath pút on his appárel, and gírd-ed

Full

hím-self with stréngth. Al - le - lú - ia.

Offertory   Tone II

Gód· hath máde the róund wórld so súre that it cán-not

be móv-ed: év-er since the wórld begán hath thy séat, O

Gód, been prepáred; thóu art from ev - er - lást-ing.

Communion   Tone I

Re - jóice gréatly, O dáughter of Síon, shóut, O dáughter

of Je - rú - sa - lem: be - hóld, thy kíng cómeth

unto thee; he is júst, and háv - ing sal - vá - tion.

663 CHRISTMAS DAY

Introit   Tone VII

Cantors

Un - to ús a Chíld is bórn; unto ús a Són is gív-

Choir

en: and the góvernment shall be upón his shóulder;

and his Náme shall be cálled, Angel of mígh- ty

FINE *Cantors*

Cóun - sel. *Ps.* O síng un-to the Lórd a néw song:

Choir   *Cantors*

for hé hath done már-vellous thíngs. Gló-ry be ... and

Choir

to the Hó - ly Ghóst. As it wás ... and év-er shǎll

Full

be: wórld with-óut énd. A - men. Un - to ús *(etc.)*

Gradual   Tone V

Cantors

All the énds of the éarth have séen the sal-vá-tion of

Choir

óur God: O be jóyful in Gód, áll ye lánds.

Cantors   *Choir*

℣. The Lórd hath declǎred his sal-vá-tion: in the síght of the

CHRISTMAS DAY (continued)

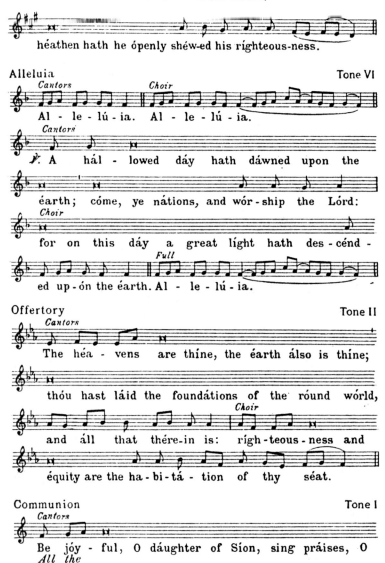

héathen hath he ópenly shéw-ed his ríghteous-ness.

Alleluia   Tone VI

Cantors   *Choir*

Al - le - lú - ia.   Al - le - lú - ia.

Cantors

℣. A   hál - lowed   dáy   hath   dáwned   upon   the

éarth;   cóme,   ye   nátions,   and wór - ship   the   Lórd:

Choir

for   on   this   dáy   a   great   líght   hath   des - cénd -

Full

ed up - ón the éarth. Al - le - lú - ia.

Offertory   Tone II

Cantors

The héa - vens   are thíne, the éarth álso is thíne;

thóu hast láid the foundátions of the róund wórld,

Choir

and áll   that   thére-in is: rígh - teous - ness and

équity are the ha - bi - tá - tion of thy séat.

Communion   Tone I

Cantors

Be   jóy - ful, O dáughter of Síon, sing práises, O
All the

Choir

dáughter of Je - rú - sa - lem: be - hóld, thy kíng
énds of the wórld: have séen the sal -

cómeth; he is ríghteous and háv - ing sal - vá - tion.
vá - tion of óur God.

664   ST. STEPHEN
Introit   Tone VII

Cantors

Prín - ces moreóver did sít, and did wítness fálsely

agáinst me, and the ungódly préssed sóre up - ón me:

Choir

O Lórd my Gód, stand úp to hélp me; for thy sérvant is

FINE

óccupied contínually in thý com - mánd - ments.

Cantors

Ps. Bléss-ed are thóse that are unde-fí - led in the wáy:

Choir   Cantors

and wálk in the láw of the Lórd. Gló-ry be....

Choir

and to the Hó-ly Ghóst. As it wás... and év- er sháll be:

Full

wórld with-óut énd. A - men. Prín - ces moreóver *(etc.)*

ST. STEPHEN (continued)

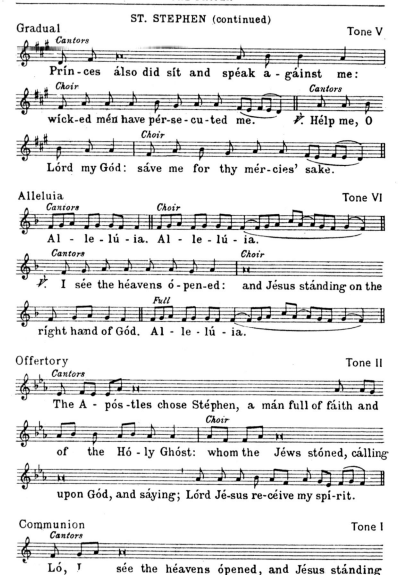

Gradual   Tone V

Cantors
Prín - ces álso did sít and spéak a - gáinst me:

Choir   *Cantors*
wíck-ed mén have pér-se-cu-ted me.   ℣. Hélp me, O

Choir
Lórd my Gód: sáve me for thy mér-cies' sake.

Alleluia   Tone VI

Cantors   *Choir*
Al - le-lú - ia. Al - le - lú - ia.

Cantors   *Choir*
℣. I sée the héavens ó-pen-ed: and Jésus stánding on the

Full
ríght hand of Gód. Al - le - lú - ia.

Offertory   Tone II

Cantors
The A - pós -tles chose Stéphen, a mán full of fáith and

Choir
of   the Hó - ly Ghóst: whom the Jéws stóned, cálling

upon Gód, and sáying; Lórd Jé-sus re-céive my spí-rit.

Communion   Tone I

Cantors
Ló, I   sée the héavens ópened, and Jésus stánding

on the right hand of the pów - er· of Gód:

Choir

O Lórd Jésus, recéive my spírit, and láy not this sín

to their chárge for they knów not whát they do.

665   ST JOHN THE EVANGELIST

Introit   Tone VII

Cantors

In the mídst of the congregátion he ópened his móuth;

and the Lórd fílled him with the spírit of wísdom and

Choir

un - der-stánd-ing: in a róbe of glóry he ar-ráy-

FINE   *Cantors*

ed him. *Ps.*A tréa-sure of jóy and gládness:
       It is a góod thing to give thánks unto the Lórd:

Choir   *Cantors*

hath he gíven him for an in-hé-ritance. Glóry be...
and to sing práises unto thy Náme, O most Hígh-est.

and to the Há-ly Ghóst. **As** ít wás... and év - er
                                        Full

shátll be: wórld with-óut énd. A - men In the mídst *(etc.)*

Gradual   ST. JOHN THE EVANGELIST (continued)   Tone V

Cantors

Then wént this sáying abróad amóng the bréthren,

Choir

that thát dis-cí - ple shóuld not díe: yet Jésus said

nót unto him; Hé shall nót die. ℣. But, If I wíll

that he tár-ry till I cóme: fól-low thou me.

Alleluia   Tone VI

Cantors   *Choir*

Al - le - lú - ia. Al - le - lú - ia.

Cantors

℣. This is the disciple which téstifieth of

Choir

thése things: and we knów that his tés - ti - mo -

Full

ny is trúe. Al - le - lú - ia.

Offertory   Tone II

Cantors

The rígh - teous shall flóu-rish like a pálm tree:

Choir

and shall spréad abróad like a cé-dar in Lí -ba - nus.

Communion   Tóne I

Cantors

Then wént abróad this sáying amóng the bréthren,

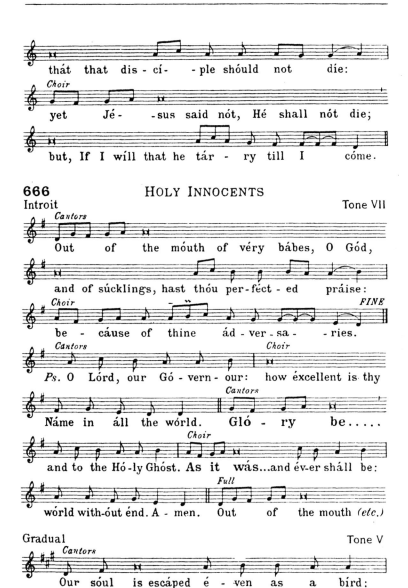

thát that dis - cí- - ple shóuld not díe:

Choir

yet Jé- -sus said nót, Hé shall nót díe;

but, If I wíll that he tár - ry till I cóme.

666   HOLY INNOCENTS

Introit   Tone VII

Cantors

Out of the móuth of véry bábes, O Gód,

and of súcklings, hast thóu per-féct - ed práise:

Choir   *FINE*

be - cáuse of thine ád - ver - sa - - ries.

Cantors   *Choir*

Ps. O Lórd, our Gó - vern - our: how éxcellent is· thy

Cantors

Náme in áll the wórld. Gló - ry be.....

Choir

and to the Hó-ly Ghóst. As it wás...and év-er sháll be:

Full

wórld with-óut énd. A - men. Out of the mouth *(etc.)*

Gradual   Tone V

Cantors

Our sóul is escáped é - ven as a bírd:

HOLY INNOCENTS (continued)

Choir *out of the snáre of the fówl-er.*   ℣. The snáre is bróken,

Choir and wé are de - lív-er - ed: our   hélp stándeth in the

Náme of the Lórd, who hath máde héa-ven and éarth.

Alleluia   Tone VI

Cantors Al - le - lú - ia. **Choir** Al - le - lú - ia.

Cantors ℣. The nó - ble ár - my of már-tyrs: práise
Práise the Lórd, ye   *chil-dren: O práise the Náme*

thee, O Lórd. Al - le - lú - ia.
of the Lórd.

If this Feast falls on a week-day, instead of the
Alleluia the following may be sung:

Tract   Tone VIII

Cantors The blóod of thy sáints have they shéd like

Choir wáter on évery síde of Je - rú - sa - lem: and thére

Cantors was nó man to bú - ry them. ℣. Avénge, O Lórd, the

Choir blóod of thy sáints: that is shéd up - ón the éarth.

Offertory   Tone II

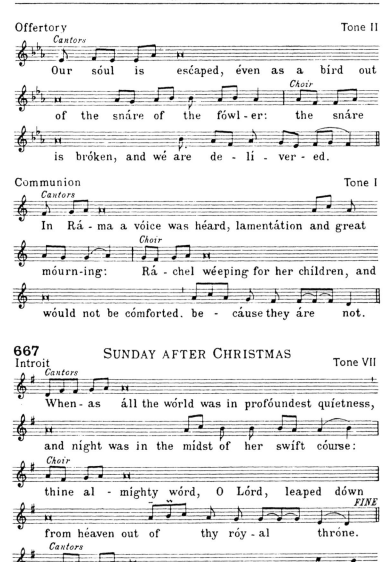

Cantors

Our sóul is escáped, éven as a bírd out of the snáre of the fówl - er: the snáre is bróken, and wé are de - lí - ver - ed.

Choir

Communion   Tone I

Cantors

In Rá - ma a vóice was héard, lamentátion and great móurn-ing: Rá - chel wéeping for her chíldren, and wóuld not be cómforted. be - cáuse they áre not.

Choir

667   SUNDAY AFTER CHRISTMAS

Introit   Tone VII

Cantors

When - as áll the wórld was in profóundest quíetness, and níght was in the mídst of her swíft cóurse: thine al - míghty wórd, O Lórd, leaped dówn from héaven out of thy róy - al thróne. *FINE*

Choir

Cantors

Ps. The Lórd is Kíng, and hath pút on gló - rious

SUNDAY AFTER CHRISTMAS (continued)

Choir

ap - pá - rel: the Lórd hath pút on his appárel, and

Cantors

gírd-ed him-sélf with stréngth. **Gló-ry be** .... and to

Choir

the Hó-ly Ghóst. **As it wás** ... and év-er shÃll be:

Full

wórld with-óut énd. A - men. When-as áll the wórld *(etc.)*

Gradual　　　　　　　　　　　　　　　　　**Tone V**

Cantors　　　　　　　　　　　*Choir*

Thóu art fáirer than the chíl-dren of mén: fúll of gráce

Cantors

are thy líps.　℣. My héart is indíting of a góod mátter;

I spéak of the thíngs which I have máde un-to the Kíng:

Choir

my tóngue is the pén of a rea-dy wrí - ter.

Alleluia　　　　　　　　　　　　　　　　　**Tone VI**

Cantors　　　　　　　*Choir*

Al - le - lú - ia. Al - le - lú - ia.

Cantors

℣. The Lórd is Kíng, and hath pút on glórious ap-pá - rel:

Choir

the Lórd hath pút on his appárel, and gírd - ed him -

Full

sélf with stréngth. Al - le - lú - ia.

Offertory   Tone II

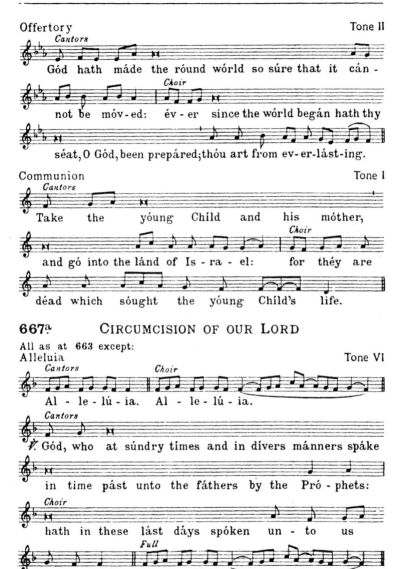

Gód hath máde the róund wórld so súre that it cán -

not be móv-ed: év-er since the wórld begán hath thy

séat, O Gód, been prepáred; thóu art from ev-er-lást-ing.

Communion   Tone I

Take the yóung Chíld and his móther,

and gó into the lánd of Is - ra - el: for théy are

déad which sóught the yóung Chíld's life.

667ª CIRCUMCISION OF OUR LORD

All as at **663** except:
Alleluia   Tone VI

Al - le - lú - ia. Al - le - lú - ia.

℣. Gód, who at súndry tímes and in dívers mánners spáke

in time pást unto the fáthers by the Pró - phets:

hath in these lást dáys spóken un - to us

by his Són. Al - le - lú - ia.

668 THE EPIPHANY

Introit   Tone VII

Cantors *Choir*
Be - hóld, he appéareth, the Lórd and Rú - ler: and in

FINE
his hánd the kíngdom, and pówer, and do - mín - ion.

Cantors *Choir*
Ps. Give the Kíng thy júdgements, O Gód: and thy ríghteousness

Cantors
un - to the Kíng's Són.   Gló - ry   be. . . . . and to the

Choir
Hó - ly Ghóst.   As   it   wás. . . . and év - er sháll be:

Full
wórld with-óut énd.   A - men.   Be - hóld, he appéareth (*etc.*)

Gradual   Tone V

Cantors
All they from Sába shall cóme, bringing góld and ín - cense:

Choir
and shall shéw forth the práis - es of   the   Lórd.

Cantors
℣. A - ríse   and   shíne,   O   Je - rú - sa - lem:

Choir
for the glóry of the Lórd is rí-sen up-on   thee.

Alleluia   Tone VI

Cantors   *Choir*

Al - le - lú - ia.   Al - le - lú - ia.

Cantors

℣. We have séen his stár in the Eást:

Choir

and are cóme with ófferings to wór - ship the Lórd.

Full

Al - le - lú - ia.

Offertory   Tone II

Cantors

The Kíngs of Thársis and of the ísles shall

give présents; the Kíngs of Arábia and Sá - ba

Choir

shall bring gífts: all Kíngs shall fall dówn

befóre him; all ná-tions shall dó him sér - vice.

Communion   Tone I

Cantors   *Choir*

We have séen his stár in the Eást: and are

cóme with our ófferings to wór - ship the Lórd.

669   EPIPHANY I

Introit   Tone VII

Cantors

On a thróne exálted I behéld, and ló, a mán sítting,

whom a légion of ángels wórship, síng-ing to-gé - ther:

Choir

be - hóld, his rúle and góvernance en-dúr - eth

FINE   *Cantors*

to all á - ges. *Ps.* O be jóy-ful in Gód, all ye lands:

Choir   *Cantors*

sérve the Lórd with glád - ness.   Gló - ry be.......

Choir

and to the Hó-ly Ghóst. As it wás... and éver sháll be:

Full

wórld withóut énd. A - men.   On a thróne exálted (*etc.*)

Gradual   Tone V

Cantors

Bléss-ed be the Lórd, éven the Gód of Is - ra - el:

Choir

which ón - ly dó - eth wón-drous things.

Cantors

℣. The móun - tains ál - so shall bring péace:

and the little hills ríghteousness un-to the péo-ple.

Alleluia　　　　　　　　　　　　　　　　　　　Tone VI

Cantors　　　　　*Choir*

Al - le - lú - ia.　Al - le - lú - ia.

Cantors　　　　　　　　　　　　*Choir*

℣. O be jóyful in the Lórd, áll ye lánds: sérve the Lórd

Full

with gládness.　Al - le - lú - ia.

Offertory　　　　　　　　　　　　　　　　　　Tone II

Cantors

O be jóy-ful in the Lórd, áll ye lánds; sérve the

Lórd with gládness, and cóme be-fóre his pré-sence

Choir

with a sóng: be ye súre that the Lórd hé is Gód.

Communion　　　　　　　　　　　　　　　　　Tone I

Cantors

Són, whý hast thóu thus déalt with us?

Behóld, thy fáther and I have sóught thee

Choir

sór - row - ing:　And he sáid unto them, Hów is

EPIPHANY I (continued)

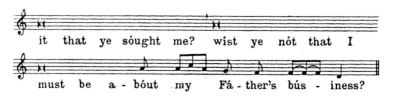

it   that   ye   sóught   me?   wist   ye   nót   that   I

must   be   a - bóut   my   Fá - ther's   bús - iness?

670   **EPIPHANY II**

Introit   Tone VII

Cantors

All   the   éarth shall wórship thée, O   Gód, and

Choir

síng   of   thee: they shall síng práise to thy Náme,

FINE   *Cantors*

O   most Hígh-est. *Ps.* O be jóy-ful in Gód, all ye lánds:

Choir

síng práises unto the   hónour   of   his   Náme;

make   his   práise   to   be   gló - ri - ous.

Cantors

Gló - ry   be . . . . . and   to   the   Hó - ly Ghóst.

Choir

As   it   wás . . . . . . and   év - er   shall   be:

Full

wórld withóut énd. A - men.   All   the   éarth (*etc.*)

Gradual   Tone V

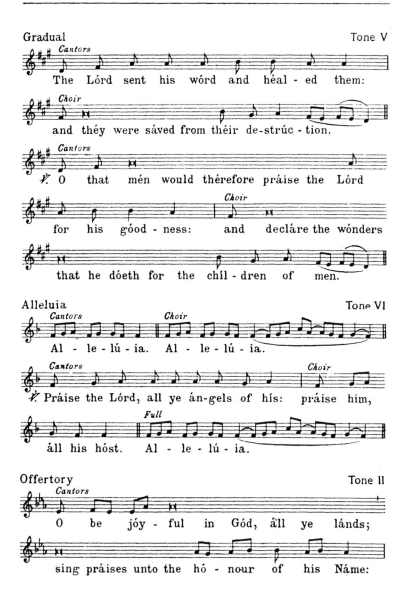

The Lórd sent his wórd and héal - ed them:

and théy were sáved from théir de-strúc - tion.

℣. O that mén would thérefore práise the Lórd

for his góod - ness: and decláre the wónders

that he dóeth for the chíl - dren of men.

Alleluia   Tone VI

Al - le - lú - ia. Al - le - lú - ia.

℣. Práise the Lórd, all ye án-gels of hís: práise him,

áll his hóst. Al - le - lú - ia.

Offertory   Tone II

O be jóy - ful in Gód, áll ye lánds;

sing práises unto the hó - nour of his Náme:

EPIPHANY II (continued)

Choir

O come híther, and héarken, all yé that fear Gód;

and I will téll you what the Lórd hath

dóne for my sóul, al - le - lú - ia.

Communion   Tone l

Cantors   *Choir*

The Lórd sáid un-to thém: Fíll the wáter-pots

with wáter, and báre unto the gó - vern -

Cantors

or of the féast. When the rúler of the féast had tásted

the wáter that was máde wine, he sáith un-to the

Choir

bríde-groom: Thou hast képt the góod wine un -

Cantors

til nów. Thís be - gín-ning of mí - ra - cles:

Choir

did Jé - sus be - fóre his dis - cí - ples.

671   Epiphany III to VI

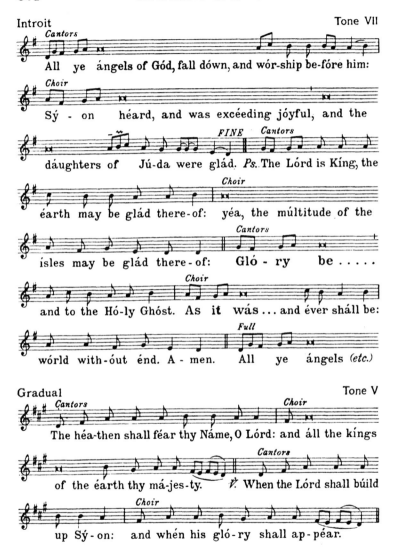

Introit   Tone VII

Cantors

All ye ángels of Gód, fall dówn, and wór-ship be-fóre him:

Choir

Sý - on héard, and was excéeding jóyful, and the

FINE   *Cantors*

dáughters of Jú-da were glád. *Ps.* The Lórd is Kíng, the

Choir

éarth may be glád there-of: yéa, the múltitude of the

Cantors

ísles may be glád there-of: Gló - ry be . . . . .

Choir

and to the Hó-ly Ghóst. As it wás . . . and éver sháll be:

Full

wórld with-óut énd. A - men. All ye ángels *(etc.)*

Gradual   Tone V

Cantors   *Choir*

The héa-then shall féar thy Náme, O Lórd: and áll the kíngs

Cantors

of the éarth thy má-jes-ty. *V.* When the Lórd shall búild

Choir

up Sý-on: and whén his gló-ry shall ap-péar.

EPIPHANY III to VI (continued)

Alleluia   Tone VI

Cantors   *Choir*

Al - le - lú - ia. Al - le - lú - ia.

Cantors

℣. The Lórd is Kíng, the éarth may be glád there-of:

Choir

yéa, the múltitude of the ísles may be glád there-of.

Full

Al - le - lú - ia.

Offertory   Tone II

Cantors

The ríght hánd of the Lórd hath the pre-éminence;

the ríght hánd of the Lórd bríng-eth mígh-ty things to páss:

Choir

I shall not díe but líve, and de-cláre the wórks of the Lórd.

Communion   Tone I

Cantors   *Choir*

All wóndered at the grácious wórds: which procéeded óut of his móuth.

672   SEPTUAGESIMA

Introit   Tone VII

Cantors

The sór-rows of déath came abóut me; the páins of héll

Choir

gat hóld up-ón me: and in my tríbulátion I máde

my práyer unto the Lórd, and he regárded my

FINE

supplicátion óut of his hó - ly tém - ple.

Cantors

Ps. I will lóve thee, O Lórd, my stréngth: the Lórd is my

Cantors

stóny róck, my fórtress, and my Sá-viour. Gló-ry be.....

Choir

and to the Hó-ly Ghóst. As it wás... and év-er sháll be:

Full

wórld with-óut énd. A-men. The sor - rows of death *(etc.)*

Gradual Tone V

Cantors

The Lórd will be a refúge in the tíme of tróuble;

and théy that knów thy Náme will pút their trúst in thée:

Choir

for thóu, Lórd, hast néver fáiled thém that séek thee.

Cantors

V. For the póor shall not álways be forgótten; the pátient

abíding of the méek shall not pé-rish for év-er:

Choir

úp, Lórd, and lét not mán have the úp-per hánd.

SEPTUAGESIMA (continued)

Tract   Tone VIII

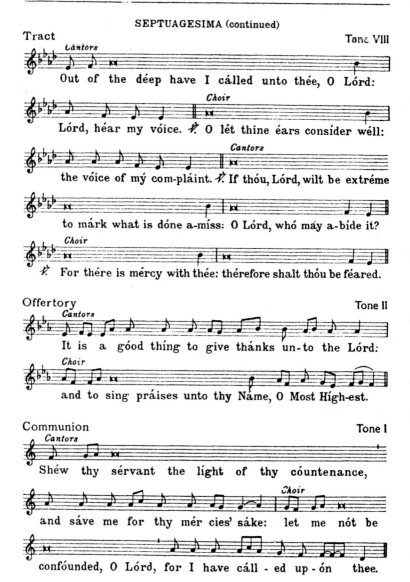

Cantors

Out of the déep have I cálled unto thée, O Lórd:

Choir

Lórd, héar my vóice. ℣. O lét thine éars consíder wéll:

Cantors

the vóice of mý com-pláint. ℣. If thóu, Lórd, wilt be extréme

to márk what is dóne a-míss: O Lórd, whó máy a-bíde it?

Choir

℣. For thére is mércy with thée: thérefore shalt thóu be féared.

Offertory   Tone II

Cantors

It is a góod thíng to give thánks un-to the Lórd:

Choir

and to sing práises unto thy Náme, O Most Hígh-est.

Communion   Tone I

Cantors

Shéw thy sérvant the líght of thy cóuntenance,

Choir

and sáve me for thy mér cies' sáke: let me nót be

confóunded, O Lórd, for I have cáll - ed up - ón thee.

673   SEXAGESIMA

Introit   Tone VII

A - ríse, O Lórd, whérefore sléepest thou? awáke, and cást

us not a-wáy for év - er: whére-fore hídest thou thy

cóuntenance, and forgéttest our advérsity and mísery?

our bélly cléaveth unto the gróund; aríse, and sáve us,

O Lórd, our hélper and our de - lí - ver - er.

Ps. O Gód, we have héard with our éars: our fá-thers have tóld us.

Glo-ry be.... and to the Hó-ly Ghóst. As it was... and év-er

sháll be: wórld with-óut énd. A-men. A - ríse, O Lórd *(etc.)*

Gradual   Tone V

Let the nátions knów that thóu, whose Náme is Je-hó-vah:

art ónly the Most Híghest ó-ver all the éarth.

SEXAGESIMA (continued)

Cantors

℣. O my Gód, make them líke un-to a whéel:

and as the stúb-ble be-fóre the wínd.

Tract   Tone VIII

Cantors

Thou hast móved the lánd, O Lórd: and di-víd-ed it.

Choir   Cantors

℣. Héal the sóres there-óf: for it shák-eth. ℣ That théy may tríumph

Choir

becáuse of the trúth: that thy belóved may be de-lív-er-ed.

Offertory   Tone II

Cantors

O hóld thou up my góings in thy páths, that my fóotsteps slíp not;

inclíne thine éar to me, and héark-en ún-to my wórds:

Choir

shéw thy márvellous lóving-kíndness, O Lórd; thóu that art

the Sáviour of thém that pút their trúst in thée.

Communion   Tone I

Cantors

I will gó un-to the ál-tar of Gód:

Choir

á - ven unto the Gód of my jóy and glád-ness.

674 QUINQUAGESIMA

Introit Tone VII

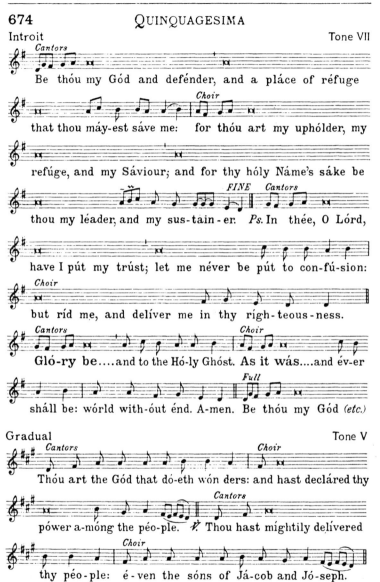

Cantors

Be thóu my Gód and defénder, and a pláce of réfuge

Choir

that thou máy-est sáve me: for thóu art my uphólder, my

refúge, and my Sáviour; and for thy hóly Náme's sáke be

FINE *Cantors*

thou my léader, and my sus-tàin - er. *Ps.* In thée, O Lórd,

have I pút my trúst; let me néver be pút to con-fú-sion:

Choir

but ríd me, and delíver me in thy rígh-teous-ness.

Cantors *Choir*

Gló-ry be....and to the Hó-ly Ghóst. As it wás....and év-er

Full

sháll be: wórld with-óut énd. A-men. Be thóu my Gód *(etc.)*

Gradual Tone V

Cantors *Choir*

Thóu art the Gód that dó-eth wón ders: and hast decláred thy

Cantors

pówer a-móng the péo-ple. *℣.* Thou hast míghtily delívered

Choir

thy péo-ple: é-ven the sóns of Já-cob and Jó-seph.

QUINQUAGESIMA (continued)

Tract Tone VIII

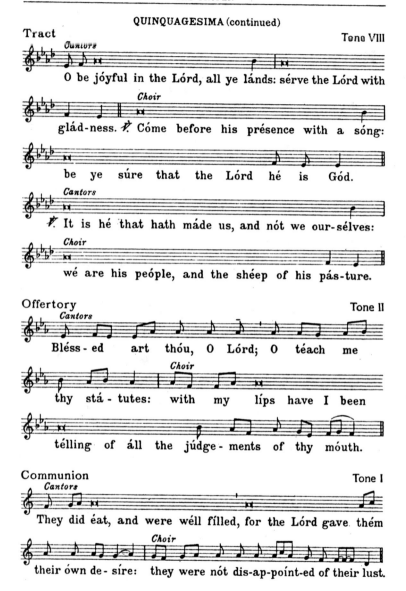

Cantors
O be jóyful in the Lórd, all ye lánds: sérve the Lórd with

Choir
glád-ness. ℣. Cóme before his présence with a sóng:

be ye súre that the Lórd hé is Gód.

Cantors
℣. It is hé that hath máde us, and nót we our-sélves:

Choir
wé are his peóple, and the sheép of his pás-ture.

Offertory Tone II

Cantors
Bléss-ed art thóu, O Lórd; O téach me

Choir
thy stá-tutes: with my líps have I been

télling of áll the júdge-ments of thy móuth.

Communion Tone I

Cantors
They did éat, and were wéll fílled, for the Lórd gave thém

Choir
their ówn de-síre: they were nót dis-ap-poínt-ed of their lust.

675   ASH-WEDNESDAY

Introit   Tone VII

Cantors

Thou hast mercy on áll things, O Lórd, and hátest nóthing

Choir

that thou hast cre-á-ted: and wínk-est at mén's iníquities,

becáuse they should aménd, and spárest áll men, for they are

FINE   *Cantors*

thíne, O Lórd, thou lóv-er of sóuls. *Ps.* Be mér-ciful unto me,

Choir

O Gód, be mér-ci-ful ún-to me: for my sóul trúst-eth in thee.

Cantors   *Choir*

Gló-ry be.... and to the Hó-ly Ghóst. As it wás....and év-er

Full

sháll be: wórld with-óut énd. A-men. Thou hast mércy *(etc.)*

Gradual   Tone V

Cantors

Be mér-ciful unto me, O God, be mér-ci-ful ún-to me:

Choir   *Cantors*

for my sóul trúst-eth in thee. ℣. He shall sénd from héa-ven:

Choir

and sáve me from the repróof of him that would éat me up.

ASH - WEDNESDAY (continued)

Tract   Tone VIII

O Lórd, deal not with us áfter our síns: nor rewárd us

according to our wíck-ed-ness-es. ℣. O Lórd, remémber nót

our óld síns, but have mércy upón us, and thát soon:

for we are cóme to gréat mí-se-ry. ℣ Hélp us, O Gód of

our salvátion, for the glóry of thy Náme, O Lórd:

O delíver us and be mérciful unto our síns, for thy Náme's sáke.

Offertory   Tone II

I will mág-nify thée, O Lórd, for thou hast sét me úp,

and nót made my fóes to trí - umph ó - ver me:

O Lórd my Gód, I críed unto thée, and thóu hast héal-ed me.

Communion   Tone I

He who doth méditate on the láw of the Lórd dáy

and níght: will bríng forth his frúit in due séa - son.

676   LENT I

Introit   Tone VII

Cantors

He — shall cáll upon me, and I will héarken unto him;

I will delíver him, and bríng him to hó - nour:

Choir   *FINE*

with léngth of dáys will I sát - is - fy him.

Cantors

Ps. Whó - so dwélleth under the defénce of the Móst Hígh:

Choir

shall abíde under the shádow of the Al - mígh - ty.

Cantors

Gló - ry be . . . . . . and to the Ho - ly Ghóst.

Choir

As it wás . . . . . and év-er shráll be: wórld with-óut

Full

énd. A - men. He — shall cáll upon me *(etc.)*

Gradual   Tone V

Cantors

He shall gíve his Ángels chárge o - ver thee:

Choir

to kéep thee in áll thy wáys.

LENT I (continued)

Cantors
℣. They shall bear thee in their hands:

Choir
that thou hurt not thy foot a-gainst a stone.

Tract   **Tone VIII**

Cantors
Who-so dwelleth under the defence of the Most High:

shall abide under the shadow of the Al-migh-ty.

Choir
℣. I will say unto the Lord, Thou art my hope

and my strong-hold: my God, in him will I trust.

Cantors
℣. For he shall deliver thee from the snare

of the hun-ter: and from the noisome pes-ti-lence.

Choir
℣. He shall defend thee under his wings: and thou shalt be

Cantors
safe under his fea-thers. ℣. His faithfulness and truth

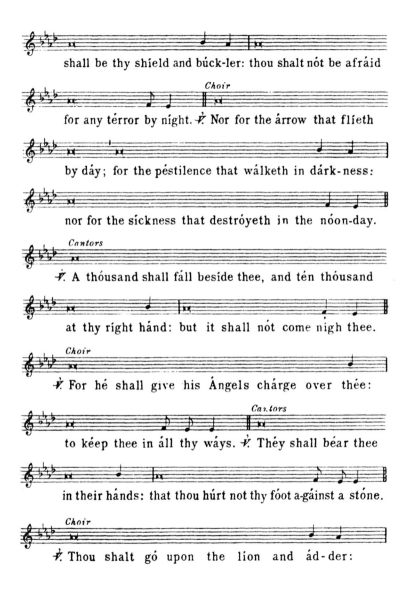

shall be thy shíeld and búck-ler: thou shalt nót be afráid

Choir

for any térror by níght. ℣. Nor for the árrow that flíeth

by dáy; for the péstilence that wálketh in dárk-ness:

nor for the síckness that destróyeth in the nóon-day.

Cantors

℣. A thóusand shall fáll besíde thee, and tén thóusand

at thy ríght hánd: but it shall nót come nígh thee.

Choir

℣. For hé shall gɪve his Ángels chárge over thée:

Cantors

to kéep thee in áll thy wáys. ℣. Théy shall béar thee

in their hánds: that thou húrt not thy fóot a-gáinst a stóne.

Choir

℣. Thou shalt gó upon the líon and ád-der:

LENT I (continued)

the young líon and the drágon shalt thou tréad under thy féet.

Cantors

℣. Becáuse he hath sét his lóve upon me, thérefore

will I de-lív-er him: I will sét him up, becáuse

he hath knówn my Náme. ℣. He shall cáll upon me,

and I will héar him: yéa, I am wíth him in troú-ble.

Cantors

℣. I will delíver him, and bríng him to hó-nour:

Choir

with lóng lífe will I sátisfy him, and shéw him my sal-vá-tion.

Offertory   Tone II

Cantors

He shall de - fénd thee únder his wíngs, and thóu shalt

Choir

be sáfe ún - der his féa-thers: his fáith-fulness

and trúth shall be thy shíeld and búck - ler.

Communion
Tone I

Cantors

Whó – so drinketh of the wáter that I shall
The Lórd shall defénd thee under his wíngs,

gíve him, sáith the Lórd:
and thóu shalt be sáfe un - der his féa - thers:

Choir

it shall bé in hím a wéll of wáter springing
his fáith-fulness and trúth shall be

up ún - to lífe e - tér - nal.
thy shíeld and búck - ler.

677 LENT II

Introit
Tone VII

Cantors

Cáll to remémbrance thy ténder compássion and

mércy, O Lórd, and thy lóving-kíndnesses towárds

Choir

us, which have been év - ér of óld: néi - ther

súffer our énemies to tríumph agáinst us; delíver us, O

FINE

Gód of Israel, out of áll our mís-e - ry and tróu - ble.

Cantors

Ps. Un - to thée, O Lórd, do I líft up my soul:

LENT II (continued)

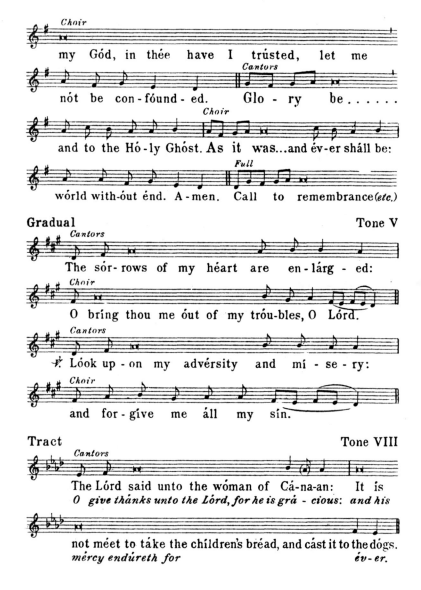

Choir
my Gód, in thée have I trústed, let me

Cantors
nót be con-fóund-ed. Glo-ry be......

Choir
and to the Hó-ly Ghóst. As it was...and év-er sháll be:

Full
wórld with-óut énd. A-men. Call to remembrance (*etc.*)

Gradual   **Tone V**

Cantors
The sór-rows of my héart are en-lárg-ed:

Choir
O bríng thou me óut of my tróu-bles, O Lórd.

Cantors
℣. Lóok up-on my advérsity and mí-se-ry:

Choir
and for-gíve me áll my sín.

Tract   **Tone VIII**

Cantors
The Lórd said unto the wóman of Cá-na-an: It ís
O give thánks unto the Lórd, for he is grá-cious: and his

not méet to táke the chíldren's bréad, and cást it to the dógs.
mércy endúreth for   év-er.

LENT II (continued)

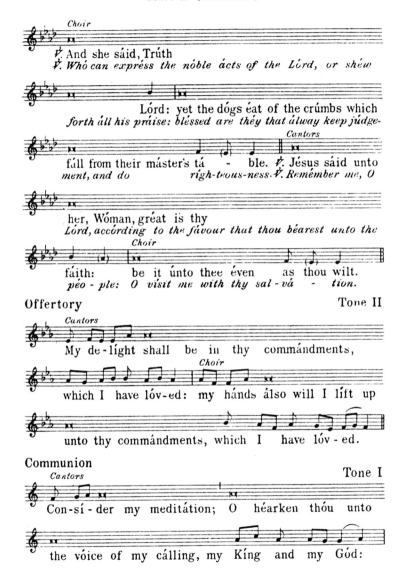

Choir

℣. And she said, Truth
℣. Who can express the noble acts of the Lord, or shew

Lord: yet the dogs eat of the crumbs which
forth all his praise: blessed are they that alway keep judge-

Cantors

fall from their master's ta - ble. ℣. Jésus said unto
ment, and do righ-teous-ness· ℣. Remember me, O

her, Woman, great is thy
Lord, according to the favour that thou bearest unto the

Choir

faith: be it unto thee even as thou wilt.
peo - ple: O visit me with thy sal - va - tion.

Offertory   Tone II

Cantors

My de - light shall be in thy commandments,

Choir

which I have lov-ed: my hands also will I lift up

unto thy commandments, which I have lov - ed.

Communion   Tone I

Cantors

Con-si - der my meditation; O hearken thou unto

the voice of my calling, my King and my God:

LENT II (continued)

Choir

for un - to thée will I máke my práyer.

678   LENT III

Introit   Tone VII

Cantors

Mine éyes are éver loóking unto the Lórd,

for hé shall plúck my féet out of the nét:

Choir

lóok thou upón me, and have mércy upón me,

FINE

for I am désolate, and in mí - se - ry.

Cantors

Ps. Un - to thée, O Lórd, do I líft up my sóul:

Choir

my Gód, in thée have I trústed, let me nót

Cantors

be con - fóund-ed. Gló - ry be . . . and to the Hó - ly

Choir

Ghóst: As it wás . . . and év - er shall be: wórld

Full

with-óut énd. A - men. Mine éyes are éver loóking *(etc.)*

● Gradual   Tone V

Cantors

Choir

Up, Lórd, and lét not mán have the úp-per hánd: let the héa-

-then be júdg-ed in thy síght. ℣. While mine é-ne-mies are

Cantors

Choir

drí-ven báck: they shall fáll and pérish at thy pré-sence.

● Tract   Tone VIII

Cantors

Un-to thée lift I úp mine éyes: O thóu that dwéllest in

Choir

the héa-vens. ℣. Behold, éven as the éyes of sér-vants:

Cantors

lóok unto the hánd of their más-ters. ℣. And as the

éyes of a máid-en: unto the hánd of her mís-tress.

Choir

℣. Éven so our éyes wáit upon the Lórd our Gód:

Cantors

until he have mércy up-ón us. ℣. Have mércy

Choir

upón us, O Lórd: have mércy up-ón us.

LENT III (continued)

Offertory   Tone II

Cantors

The stá-tutes of the Lórd are right, and re - jóice

Choir

the héart: swéet-er also than hóney and the hóneycomb;

moreover by thém is thy sér - vant táught.

Communion   Tone I

Cantors

The spár-row hath fóund her an hóuse, and the swállow

Choir

a nést where shé may láy her yóung: év- en thy áltars,

Cantors

O Lórd of hósts, my Kíng and my Gód. Bléss-ed are théy that

Choir

dwéll in thy hóuse: théy will be ál - way práis-ing thee.

679   LENT IV

Introit   Tone VII

Cantors

Re - jóice ye with Jerúsalem; and be ye

glád for her, áll ye that de-líght in her:

Choir

ex - últ and sing for jóy with her, all yé that in

sádness móurn for her; that yé may súck, and be

FINE

sátisfied with the bréasts of her con-so-lá - tions.

Cantors .... *Choir*

Ps. I was gláad when they sáid un-to me: We will gó

Cantors

into the hóuse of the Lórd. Gló-ry be.... and to

Choir

the Hó - ly Ghóst. As it wás... and ev-er sháll be:

Full

wórld with-óut énd. A men. Re - jóice ye *(etc.)*

Gradual Tone V

Cantors .... *Choir*

I was gláad when they sáid un-to me: we will gó into the

Cantors

house of the Lord. ℣. Péace be with-ín thy wálls:

Choir

and plénteousness with-ín thy pá-la-ces.

Tract Tone VIII

Cantors

They that pút their trúst in the Lórd, shall be

éven as the móunt Sý-on: which máy not be remóved,

LENT IV (continued)

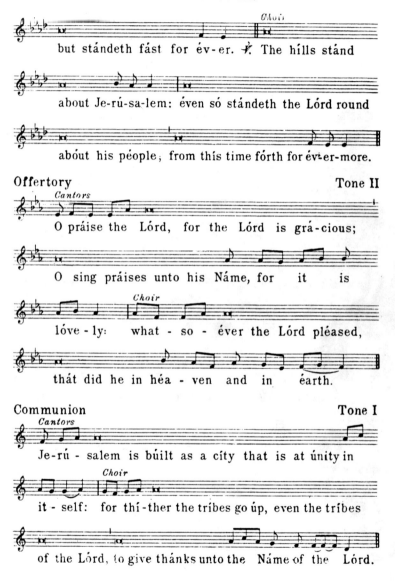

but stándeth fást for év-er. ℣. The hílls stánd

about Je-rú-sa-lem: éven só stándeth the Lórd round

abóut his péople; from thís time fórth for év‐er-more.

Offertory   Tone II

Cantors

O práise the Lórd, for the Lórd is grá-cious;

O sing práises unto his Náme, for   it   is

Choir

lóve - ly: what - so - éver the Lórd pléased,

thát did he in héa - ven and in éarth.

Communion   Tone I

Cantors

Je-rú - salem is búilt as a cíty that is at únity in

Choir

it - self: for thí-ther the tríbes go úp, even the tríbes

of the Lórd, to give thánks unto the Náme of the Lórd.

680   PASSION SUNDAY

Introit   Tone VII

Cantors

Give sén-tence with me, O Gód, and defénd the cáuse

Choir

of my sóul agáinst the un-gód-ly péo-ple: de-lí-ver me,

and ríd me from the decéitful and wícked mán; for

FINE

thóu, O Lórd, art my Gód, and my stróng sal-vá - tion.

Cantors

Ps. O sénd out thy líght and thy trúth, that théy may

Choir

léad me: and bríng me unto thy hóly híll, and

Full

to thy dwéll-ing. Give   sén-tence with me *(etc.)*

Gradual   Tone V

Cantors   *Choir*

De-lív-er me, O Lórd, from mine é-ne-mies: téach me

Cantors

to dó the thíng that pléa-seth thee. *V.* It is the Lórd that

delívereth me from my crúel énemies, and sétteth me up abóve

Choir

mine ád-ver-sa-ries: thou shalt delíver me from the wíck-ed mán.

PASSION SUNDAY (continued)

Tract   Tono VIII

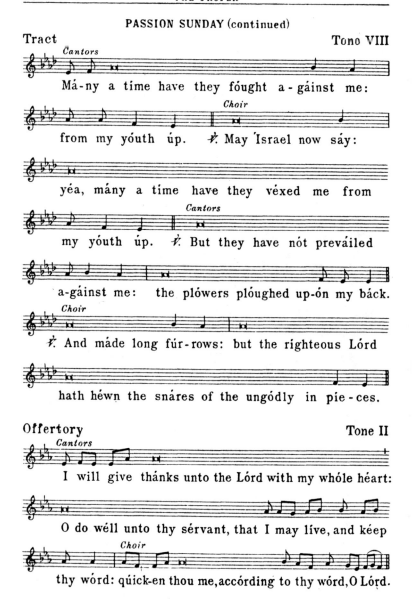

Cantors

Má-ny a time have they fóught a - gáinst me:

Choir

from my yóuth úp.   ℣. May Ísrael now sáy:

yéa, mány a time have they véxed me from

Cantors

my yóuth úp.   ℣. But they have nót preváiled

a-gáinst me: the plówers plóughed up-ón my báck.

Choir

℣. And máde long fúr-rows: but the ríghteous Lórd

hath héwn the snáres of the ungódly in pie - ces.

Offertory   Tone II

Cantors

I will give thánks unto the Lórd with my whóle héart:

O do wéll unto thy sérvant, that I may líve, and kéep

Choir

thy wórd: qúick-en thou me, accórding to thy wórd, O Lórd.

Communion   Tone I

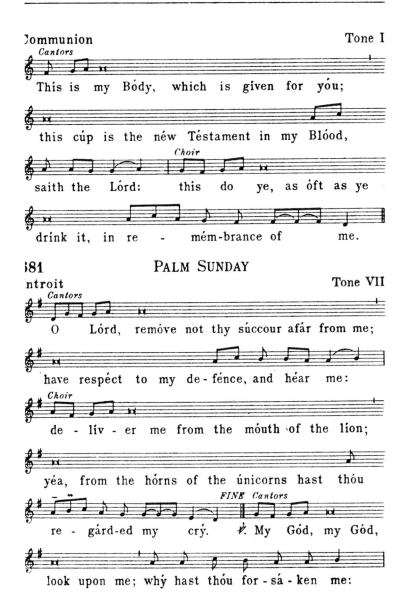

Cantors

This is my Bódy, which is gíven for yóu;

this cúp is the néw Téstament in my Blóod,

Choir

saith the Lórd: this do ye, as óft as ye

drínk it, in re - mém-brance of me.

681   PALM SUNDAY

Introit   Tone VII

Cantors

O Lórd, remóve not thy súccour afár from me;

have respéct to my de - fénce, and héar me:

Choir

de - lív - er me from the móuth of the líon;

yéa, from the hórns of the únicorns hast thóu

FINE Cantors

re - gárd-ed my crý. ℣. My Gód, my Gód,

look upon me; whý hast thóu for - sá - ken me:

PALM SUNDAY (continued)

Choir

and art so fár from my héalth, and from the wórds

Full

of my com-pláint.   O   Lórd. remóve not (*etc.*)

Gradual   **Tone V**

Cantors   *Choir*

Thou hast hólden me by my ríght hánd: thou

shalt gúide me with thy cóunsel, and áfter thát recéive

me with gló - ry.   *Cantors*   ℣. Trú-ly Gód is lóving

Choir

un - to Ís - ra - el: év - en unto súch as áre

Cantors

of a cléan héart.   Név-er-the-less, my féet

Choir

were ál-most góne: my tréad-ings had wéll nigh slípt.

Cantors

And— whý, I was grieved at the wíck - ed:

Choir

I do álso sée the ungódly in súch pros-pé-ri-ty.

Tract   Tone VIII

My Gód, my Gód, lóok upon me: whý hast thou for-

-sá-ken me? ℣. And árt so fár from my héalth:

and from the wórds of my com-pláint? ℣. O my

Gód, I crý in the dáytime, but thou héarest nót:

and in the níght season álso I táke no rést.

℣. And thóu contínuest hó-ly: O thou wórship of

'Is-ra-el. Our fáthers hóped in thée:

they trústed in thee, and thou dídst de-lív-er them.

℣. They cálled upon thee, and were hól-pen:

they pút their trúst in thée, and were nót con-fóund-ed.

PALM SUNDAY (continued)

Cantors

℣. But ás for mé, I am a wórm, and nó man:

a véry scórn of mén, and the óutcast of the

Choir

péo - ple. ℣. All they that sée me láugh me to

scórn: they shóot out their líps, and sháke their héads,

Cantors

say - ing; ℣. He trústed in Gód, that hé would de -

- lív - er him: lét him delíver him, if hé will

Choir

háve him. ℣ They stand stáring and lóoking upon me:

they párt my gárments amóng them, and cást

Cantors

lóts upon my vés - ture. ℣. Sáve me from the líon's

móuth: thou hast héard me álso from amóng the

Choir

hórns of the ú - ni - corns. ℣. O práise the Lórd, ye

that féar him: mágnify him, áll ye of the

Cantors

séed of 'Já - cob. ℣ They shall be cóunted

unto the Lórd for a gene - rá - tion:

they shall cóme, and the héavens shall decláre his

Choir

right - eous - ness. ℣. Unto a péople that

sháll be bórn: whom the Lórd hath máde.

Offertory   Tone II

Cantors

Thy re - búke hath bróken my héart, I am fúll

of héaviness: I lóoked for sóme to have píty on me,

Choir

but there was nó man: néi - ther fóund I ány to

cómfort me; they gáve me gáll to éat, and whén

I was thírsty they gáve me ví - ne -gar to drínk.

PALM SUNDAY (continued)

Communion   Tone I

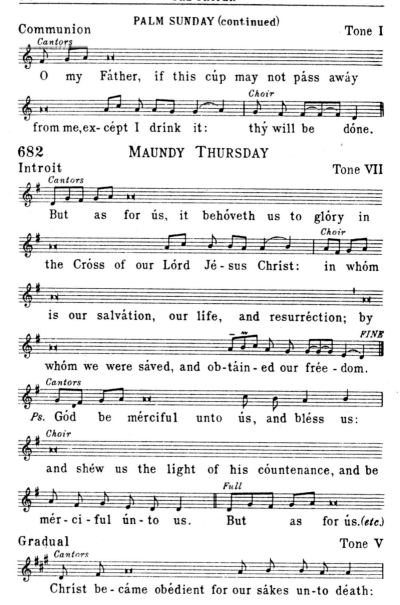

O my Fáther, if this cúp may not páss awáy

from me, ex-cépt I drínk it: thý will be dóne.

682   MAUNDY THURSDAY

Introit   Tone VII

But as for ús, it behóveth us to glóry in

the Cróss of our Lórd Jé-sus Chríst: in whóm

is our salvátion, our lífe, and resurréction; by

whóm we were sáved, and ob-táin-ed our frée-dom.

Ps. Gód be mérciful unto ús, and bléss us:

and shéw us the light of his cóuntenance, and be

mér-ci-ful ún-to us. But as for ús. *(etc.)*

Gradual   Tone V

Chríst be-cáme obédient for our sákes un-to déath:

Choir

év - en the déath of the Cróss.

Cantors

℣ Whére-fore God álso hath hígh-ly ex - ált - ed him:

Choir

and gíven him the Náme which is a-bóve év-ery náme.

There is neither Alleluia *nor* Tract *on Maundy Thursday*

Offertory   Tone II

Cantors

The ríght hand of the Lórd hath the pre-éminence;

the ríght hand of the Lórd bríng-eth mígh-ty things to páss:

Choir

I shall not díe, but líve, and de-cláre the wórks of the Lórd.

Communion   Tone I

Cantors

The Lórd Jésus, áfter that he had súpped with his discíples,

Choir

and had wáshed their féet, sáid un-to thém: Knów ye whát

I your Lórd and Máster have dóne to you? I have gíven you

an exámple, that yé should dó as I have dóne un - to you.

(682)   Invention of the Cross

Introit   Tone VII

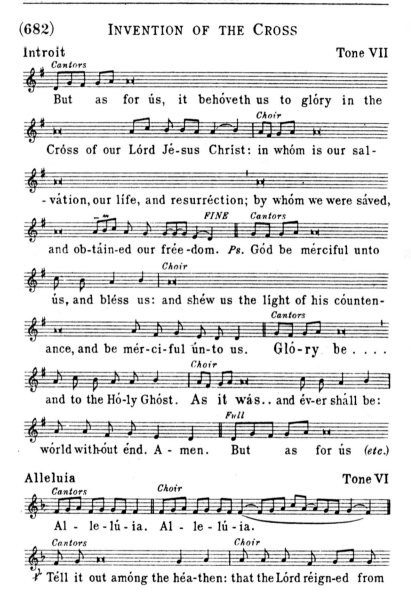

Cantors

But   as   for ús,   it behóveth us   to   glóry   in   the

Choir

Cróss of our Lórd Jé-sus Chríst: in whóm is our sal-

- vátion, our lífe, and resurréction; by whóm we were sáved,

FINE   *Cantors*

and ob-táin-ed our frée-dom. *Ps.* Gód be mérciful unto

Choir

ús, and bléss us: and shéw us the light of his cóunten-

Cantors

ance, and be mér-ci-ful ún-to us.   Gló-ry   be . . . .

Choir

and to the Hó-ly Ghóst.   As   it   wás.. and év-er shȧll be:

Full

wórld with-óut énd. A - men.   But   as   for ús   *(etc.)*

Alleluia   Tone VI

Cantors   *Choir*

Al - le - lú - ia.   Al - le - lú - ia.

Cantors   *Choir*

℣ Téll it out amóng the héa-then: that the Lórd réign-ed from

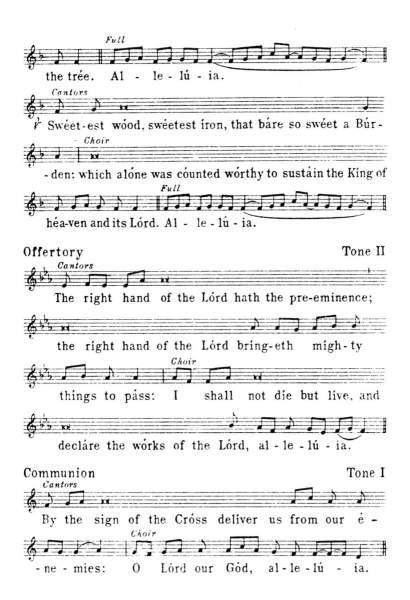

the trée. Al - le - lú - ia.

℣ Swéet-est wóod, swéetest íron, that báre so swéet a Búr-

-den: which alóne was cóunted wórthy to sustáin the Kíng of

héa-ven and its Lórd. Al - le - lú - ia.

Offertory   Tone II

The right hand of the Lórd hath the pre-eminence;

the ríght hand of the Lórd bríng-eth   mígh-ty

things to páss: I   shall not díe but líve, and

decláre the wórks of the Lórd, al - le - lú - ia.

Communion   Tone I

By the sign of the Cróss delíver us from our é -

-ne - mies: O Lórd our Gód, al - le - lú - ia.

(682)   HOLY CROSS DAY

Introit (*as on the Invention of the Cross*)
Gradual (*as on Maundy Thursday*)

Alleluia   Tone VI

Cantors   *Choir*

Al - le - lú - ia.   Al - le - lú - ia.

Cantors

℣. Swéet-est wóod, swéetest íron, that báre so swéet a Búr-den:

Choir

which ónly was cóunted wórthy to sustáin the Kíng of

Full

héa-ven and its Lórd.   Al - le - lú - ia.

Offertory   Tone II

Cantors

By the sígn of the hóly Cróss, defénd, O Lórd, thy

Choir

péople from áll the snáres of our é - ne-mies: that

the sérvice which we rénder may be pléasing unto thee,

and our sácrifice accéptable in thy síght, al-le-lú-ia.

Communion   Tone I

Cantors

By the sign of the Cróss delíver us from

Choir

our é - ne - mies;   O   Lórd   our   Gód.

(682)   GOOD FRIDAY

There is neither Introit *nor* Gradual *on Good Friday*

Tract   Tone VIII

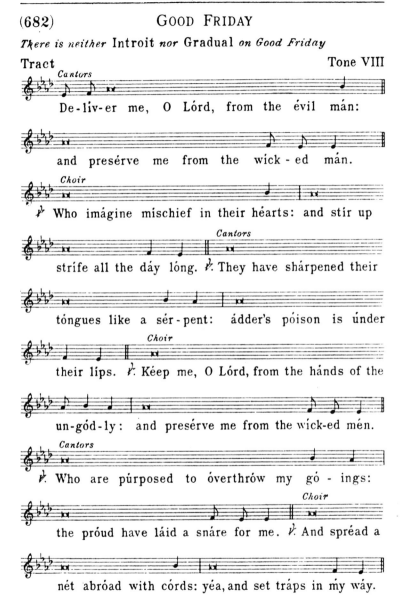

De-liv-er me, O Lórd, from the évil mán:

and presérve me from the wick-ed mán.

℣ Who imágine míschief in their héarts: and stír up

strífe all the dáy lóng. ℣. They have shárpened their

tóngues like a sér-pent: ádder's póison is únder

their líps. ℣. Kéep me, O Lórd, from the hánds of the

un-gód-ly: and presérve me from the wíck-ed mén.

℣. Who are púrposed to óverthrów my gó - ings:

the próud have láid a snáre for me. ℣. And spréad a

nét abróad with córds: yéa, and set tráps in my wáy.

GOOD FRIDAY (continued)

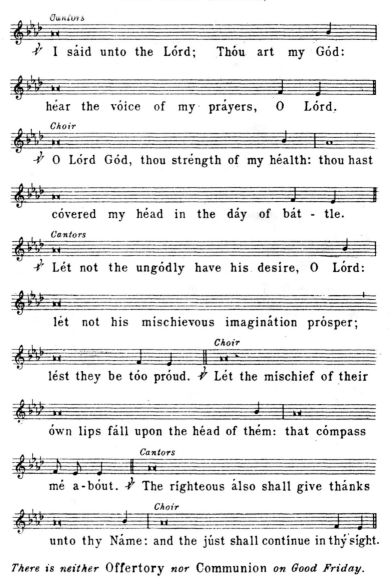

Cantors
℣ I said unto the Lórd;   Thóu art my Gód:

héar the vóice of my práyers, O Lórd.

Choir
℣ O Lórd Gód, thou stréngth of my héalth: thou hast

cóvered my héad in the dáy of bát - tle.

Cantors
℣ Lét not the ungódly have his desíre, O Lórd:

lét not his mischievous imaginátion prósper;

Choir
lést they be tóo próud. ℣ Lét the míschief of their

ówn lips fáll upon the héad of thém: that cómpass

Cantors
mé a-bóut. ℣ The ríghteous álso shall give thánks

Choir
unto thy Náme: and the júst shall contínue in thý sight.

There is neither Offertory *nor* Communion *on Good Friday.*

683   EASTER DAY

Introit   Tone VII

I am risen, and am still with thee, allelúia;

thou hast láid thine hánd upón me, al - le - lú - ia:

thy knów-ledge is tóo wónderful and éxcellent

for me, alle - lú - ia,   al - le - lú - ia.

Ps. O Lórd, thou hast séarched me óut, and knówn me:

thou knówest my dówn-sitting, and mine up - rís - ing.

Gló - ry be . . . . and to the Hó - ly Ghóst.

As it wás . . . and év- er shάll be   wórld with -

- óut énd A - men   I   am   rísen   *(etc.)*

EASTER DAY (continued)

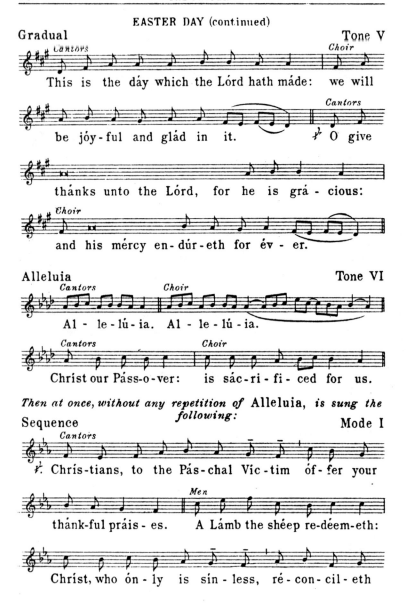

Gradual   Tone V

Cantors   *Choir*

This is the dáy which the Lórd hath máde: we will

be jóy-ful and glád in   it.   *Cantors* ℣ O give

thánks unto the Lórd,   for   he is grá - cious:

Choir

and his mércy en - dúr-eth for év - er.

Alleluia   Tone VI

Cantors   *Choir*

Al - le - lú - ia.   Al - le - lú - ia.

Cantors   *Choir*

Chríst our Páss-o-ver: is sác-ri - fi - ced for us.

Then at once, without any repetition of **Alleluia**, *is sung the following:*

Sequence   Mode I

Cantors

℣. Chrís-tians, to the Pás-chal Víc-tim   óf - fer your

Men

thánk-ful práis - es.   A Lámb the shéep re-déem-eth:

Chríst, who ón - ly   is   sín - less, ré - con - cil - eth

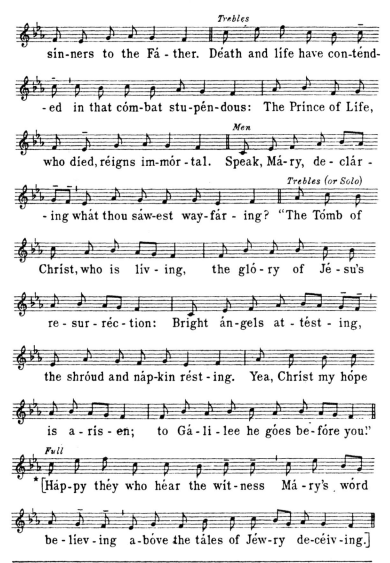

sin-ners to the Fá - ther. Déath and lífe have con-ténd-ed in that cóm-bat stu-pén-dous: The Prínce of Life, who díed, réigns im-mór -tal. Speak, Má- ry, de - clár - ing what thou sáw-est way-fár - ing? "The Tómb of Chríst, who is lív - ing, the gló - ry of Jé - su's re - sur - réc - tion: Bright án-gels at - tést - ing, the shróud and náp-kin rést - ing. Yea, Chríst my hópe is a - rís - en; to Gá - li - lee he góes be-fóre you." *[Háp-py théy who héar the wít - ness Má - ry's wórd be - líev - ing a-bóve the táles of Jéw-ry de-céiv-ing.]

*The words in square brackets are now omitted from the Western Rite.

EASTER DAY (continued)

Full

Christ in-déed from déath is rís - en,   our new
life ob-táin-ing.   Have mér-cy,   víc-tor Kíng,
év-er reign-ing!   A - men.   Al-le-lú-ia.

Offertory   **Tone II**

Cantors   *Choir*

The éarth trém-bled and was still: when Gód
a-róse to júdge-ment, al - le-lú - ia.

Communion   **Tone I**

Cantors

Christ our   Pássover is sácrificed for ús, al - le-

Choir

- lú - ia: thére-fore   let us kéep the feast with
the unléavened bréad of sincérity and trúth,
allelúia, alle-lú - ia,   al - le-lú - ia.

684 ❊   LOW SUNDAY
Introit   Tone VII

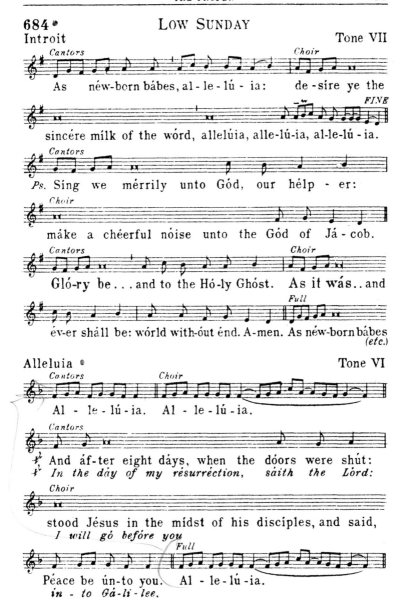

As new-born babes, al-le-lú-ia: de-sire ye the
sincére milk of the wórd, allelúia, alle-lú-ia, al-le-lú-ia.

Ps. Sing we mérrily unto Gód, our hélp - er:
máke a chéerful nóise unto the Gód of Já-cob.

Gló-ry be... and to the Hó-ly Ghóst. As it wás.. and
év-er shall be: world with-óut énd. A-men. As new-born babes
(etc.)

Alleluia ❊   Tone VI

Al - le - lú - ia. Al - le - lú - ia.

℣ And áf-ter eight days, when the dóors were shút:
℣ *In the day of my resurréction, saith the Lórd:*
stood Jésus in the mídst of his discíples, and said,
I will gó befóre you
Péace be ún-to you. Al - le - lú - ia.
in - to Gá-li-lee.

LOW SUNDAY (continued)

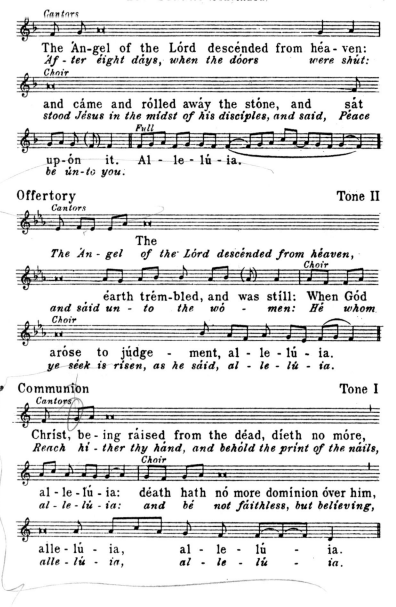

Cantors

The An-gel of the Lord descended from hea-ven:
Af - ter eight days, when the doors   were shut:

Choir

and came and rolled away the stone, and   sat
stood Jésus in the midst of his disciples, and said,   Péace

Full

up-on   it.   Al - le - lú - ia.
be un-to you.

Offertory   **Tone II**

Cantors

The
The An - gel   of the Lord descénded from héaven,

Choir

earth trém-bled, and was still: When God
and said un - to   the   wó - men: Hé   whom

Choir

aróse to júdge - ment, al - le - lú - ia.
ye séek is risen, as he said, al - le - lú - ia.

Communion   **Tone I**

Cantors

Christ, be - ing ráised from the déad, díeth no móre,
Reach hi - ther thy hánd, and behóld the print of the náils,

Choir

al - le - lú - ia: déath hath nó more domínion óver him,
al - le - lú - ia: and   bé   not fáithless, but belíeving,

alle - lú - ia,   al - le - lú - ia.
alle - lú - ia,   al - le - lú - ia.

685   EASTER II
Introit   Tone VII

Cantors
The lóv - ing- kíndness of the Lórd fílleth the

Choir
whóle wórld, al - le - lú - ia: by the wórd of the

Lórd the héavens were stáblished, alle - lú - ia,

FINE Cantors
al - le - lú - ia.   *Ps.* Re - jóice in the Lórd,

Choir
O ye ríght - eous: for it becómeth wéll the

Cantors
júst to be thánk - ful   Gló-ry be... and to the

Choir
Hó - ly Ghóst.   As it wás... and év-er sháll be

Full
wórld with-óut énd: A - men.   The lóv - ing kíndness *(etc.)*

Alleluia   Tone VI

Cantors   *Choir*
Al - le - lú - ia. Al - le- lú - ia.

EASTER II (continued)

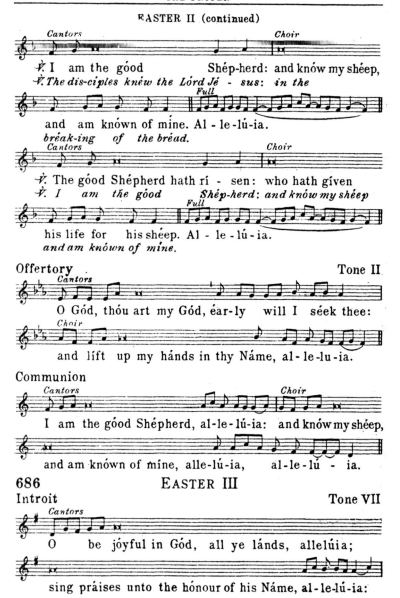

Cantors — *Choir*

℣. I am the góod Shép-herd: and knów my shéep,
℣. The dis-ci-ples knéw the Lórd Jé - sus: in the

and am knówn of míne. Al - le -lú-ia.
bréak-ing of the bréad.

Cantors — *Choir*

℣. The góod Shépherd hath rí - sen: who hath gíven
℣. I am the góod Shép-herd: and knów my shéep

his life for his shéep. Al - le - lú - ia.
and am knówn of míne.

Offertory   **Tone II**

Cantors

O Gód, thóu art my Gód, éar-ly will I séek thee:

Choir

and líft up my hánds in thy Náme, al - le -lu -ia.

Communion

Cantors — *Choir*

I am the góod Shépherd, al-le-lú-ia: and knów my shéep,

and am knówn of míne, alle-lú-ia, al-le-lú - ia.

686   E A S T E R I I I

Introit   **Tone VII**

Cantors

O be jóyful in Gód, all ye lánds, allelúia;

sing práises unto the hónour of his Náme, al-le-lú-ia:

Choir

make his práise to be excéeding glórious, allelúia,

FINE *Cantors*

alle-lú-ia   al-le-lú - ia. *Ps.* Sáy un - to Gód,

O how wónderful art thóu in thy wórks, O Lórd:

Choir   *Cantors*

through the gréat-ness of thy pów-er. Gló-ry be. . . .

Choir

and to the Hó-ly Ghóst. As it was....and év-er sháll be:

Full

wórld with-óut énd. A-men.   O   be jóyful in Gód, *(etc.)*

Alleluia   Tone VI

Cantors   *Choir*

Al - le - lú - ia. Al - le - lú - ia.

Cantors

℣. A   lít - tle whíle, and yé shall nót sée me, sáith
℣. *The Lórd hath sént re-*

Choir

the Lórd Jé - sus: and agáin, a líttle whíle and ye
démp-tion: un-

sháll see me, becáuse I gó to the   Fá - ther.
to   his   péo - ple.

EASTER III (continued)

Full

Al - le - lú - ia.

Cantors

℣. But I will sée you agáin,
℣. Ought not Christ to have

Choir

and your héart shall re - joíce:
súf-fered these things:

and your jóy no man
and to have éntered in-

Full

ták-eth fróm you. Al - le - lú - ia.
-to his glo - ry.

Offertory — Tone II

Cantors

Práise the Lórd, O my sóul; while I líve will I

Choir

práise the Lórd: yéa, as lóng as I have ány béing,

I will sing práises únto my Gód, al - le - lú - ia.

Communion — Tone 1

Cantors

A lít - tle whíle, and yé shall nót see me, al - le - lú - ia:

Choir

and a - gáin, a líttle whíle and ye sháll see me,

becáuse I gó to the Fáther, alle-lú-ia, al - le - lú - ia.

687 E ASTER IV·

Introit

Cantors

O sing unto the Lórd a néw sóng, alleluia;

for the Lórd hath done márvellous things al-le-lú-ia:

Choir

in the síght of the nátions hath he shéwed his ríghteous

FINE

júdgments, alle-lú-ia, al-le-lú - ia.

Cantors

Ps. With his ówn right hánd, and with his hó-ly árm:

Choir   *Cantors*

hath he gótten him-sélf the víc-to-ry. **Gló-ry be**.....

Choir

and to the Hó-ly Ghóst. **As it wás**... and év-er sháll be:

Full

wórld with-óut énd. A-men. O sing unto the Lórd *(etc.)*

Alleluia   Tone VI

Cantors   *Choir*

Al - le-lú-ia. Al - le-lú - ia.

EASTER IV (continued)

℣. I go to him that sent me:
℣. The right hand of the Lord hath the pre-em-i - nence:

but because I have said these things unto you,
the right hand of the Lord bringeth

sorrow hath fill-ed your hearts. Al - le - lú-ia.
mighty things to pass.

℣. I tell you the truth:
℣. Christ, be-ing raised from the dead, dieth no more:

it is expedient for you that I go a-way.
death hath no more do - min - ion o - ver him.

Al le - lú - ia.

Offertory Tone II

O be joy - ful in God all ye lands; sing praises

unto the ho - nour of his Name: O come hither,

and hearken, all ye that fear God, and I will tell

you what things he hath done for my soul, al - le-lú -ia.

Communion   Tone I

Cantors

When the Cómforter, the Spírit of Trúth, is cóme;

Choir

he will re-próve the wórld of sin: and of ríghteous-

-ness, and of júdgement, alle-lú-ia, al-le-lú - ia.

688   EASTER V

Introit   Tone VII

Cantors

With a vóice of sínging decláre ye thís,

and lét it be héard, al - le - lú - ia:

Choir

út - ter it éven unto the énds of the éarth;

the Lórd hath delívered his péople, alle-lú - ia,

FINE *Cantors*

al-le-lú - ia.   *Ps.* O be jóy-ful in Gód, áll

Choir

ye lánds: sing práises unto the hónour of his

Náme; make his práise to be gló - ri - ous.

EASTER V (continued)

Cantors

Gló - ry   be..... and to   the Hó - ly Ghóst.

Choir

As it wás   and év-er shall be: wórld with-óut énd.

Full

A - men.   With   a   vóice of sínging (etc.)

Alleluia   Tone VI

Cantors   Choir

Al - le - lú - ia. Al - le - lú - ia.

Cantors

℣. Hí - ther-to have ye asked nóthing in my Náme:
℣. Christ is rísen, and hath shéwed líght un-to ús:

Choir

ásk,   and yé shall re - céive.
whóm he hath redéemed with his most pré-cious Blóod.

Full   Cantors

Al - le - lú - ia.   ℣. Chríst, be -
                         ℣. I   came

-ing ráised from the déad,   dí - eth
fórth from the Fáther, and am cóme in - to

Choir

no móre: déath hath nó more do - mín - ion
the wórld: agáin, I léave the wórld and gó to the

Full

ó -ver him. Al - le - lú - ia.
Fá - ther.

Offertory   Tone II

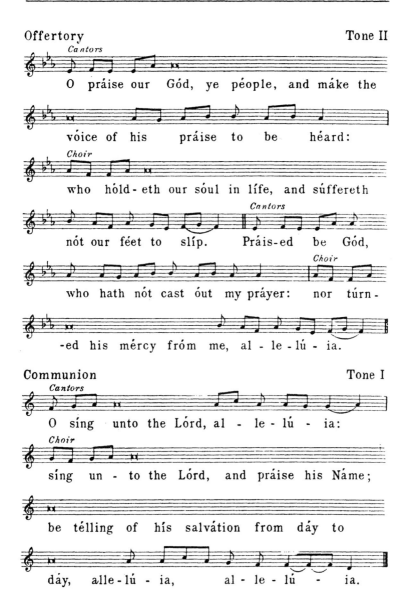

Cantors

O práise our Gód, ye péople, and máke the

vóice of his práise to be héard:

Choir

who hóld- eth our sóul in lífe, and súffereth

Cantors

nót our féet to slíp. Práis-ed be Gód,

Choir

who hath nót cast óut my práyer: nor túrn-

-ed his mércy fróm me, al - le - lú - ia.

Communion   Tone I

Cantors

O síng unto the Lórd, al - le - lú - ia:

Choir

síng un - to the Lórd, and práise his Náme;

be télling of hís salvátion from dáy to

dáy, alle - lú - ia, al - le - lú - ia.

688ᵃ ROGATION DAYS

Introit Tone VII

Cantors

He hath héard my vóice out of his hóly témple,

Choir

al - le - lú - ia: and my compláint hath cóme befóre him,

it hath éntered éven into his éars, alle-

FINE *Cantors*

- lú - ia, al - le - lú - ia. *Ps.* I will lóve thee,

Choir

O Lórd my stréngth: the Lórd is my stóny róck,

Cantors

my fórtress, and my sá - viour. Gló-ry be.... and

Choir

to the Hó-ly Ghóst. As it wás.... and év - er

Full

sháll be: wórld with-óut énd. A-men. He hath héard *(etc)*

Alleluia Tone VI

Cantors *Choir*

Al - le - lú - ia. Al - le - lú - ia.

Cantors

℣. O give thanks unto the Lórd, for hé is grá - cious:

Choir   *Full*

and his mércy en-dúr-eth for év-er. Al-le-lú-ia.

Offertory   Tone II

Cantors

I will give gréat thánks unto the Lórd with my móuth:

Choir

and práise him a-móng the múl-ti-tude.

Cantors

For hé shall stánd at the ríght hand of the póor:

Choir

to sáve his sóul from unríghteous júd-ges, al-le-lú-ia.

Communion   Tone I

Cantors

Ask, and it shall be gíven unto you;

Choir

séek, and ye shall fínd: knóck, and it shall be

Cantors

ó-pen-ed un-to you. For év-ery óne that ásketh,

Choir

recéiveth, and hé that séek-eth fínd-eth: and to

hím that knócketh, it shall be ó-pen-ed, al-le-lú-ia.

689   ASCENSION DAY

Introit   Tone VII

Cantors

Ye mén of Gálilee, why stánd ye gázing úp into

Choir

héaven? al - le-lú-ia: in líke mánnèr as ye have séen

him góing up into héaven, só shall he cóme agáin,

FINE

allelúia, alle - lú - ia, al - le - lú - ia.

Cantors

Ps. And whíle they lóoked stéadfastly towárd héaven,
Ps. O clàp your hànds togéther,

Choir

as he wént úp: behóld, two men stood bý them
àll ye péo - ple: *O sìng unto Gòd with the*

in whíte appárel, which sáid un - to them.
vòice of mè - lo - dy.

Cantors

Gló - ry be . . . . and to the Hó-ly Ghóst.

Choir

As it wás . . . . . and év- er sháll be:

Full

wórld with-óut énd. A - men. Ye mén of Gálilee (*etc.*

Alleluia   Tone VI

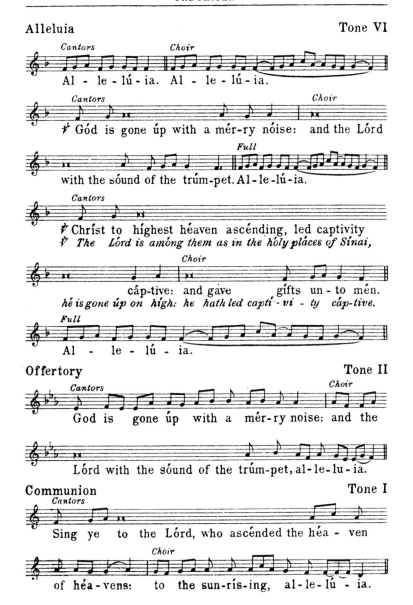

Cantors   *Choir*

Al - le - lú - ia. Al - le - lú - ia.

Cantors   *Choir*

℣ Gód is gone úp with a mér-ry nóise: and the Lórd

Full

with the sóund of the trúm-pet. Al-le-lú-ia.

Cantors

℣ Chríst to highest héaven ascénding, led captivity
℣ *The Lórd is amóng them as in the hóly pláces of Sínai,*

Choir

cáp-tive: and gáve gífts un - to mén.
hé is gone úp on hígh: he hath led capti´ - vi - ty cáp-tive.

Full

Al - le - lú - ia.

Offertory   Tone II

Cantors   *Choir*

God is gone úp with a mér-ry noise: and the

Lórd with the sóund of the trúm-pet, al-le-lu-ia.

Communion   Tone I

Cantors

Sing ye to the Lórd, who ascénded the héa - ven

Choir

of héa-vens: to the sun-rís-ing, al-le-lú - ia.

690   SUNDAY AFTER ASCENSION DAY

Introit   Tone VII

Cantors

Con - sí - der, O Lórd, and héar me, when I crý unto thee,

allelúia; unto thée my héart hath sáid, Thy fáce, Lórd,

Choir

have I sóught; thy fáce, Lórd, will I séek: O híde not thóu

FINE

thy fáce from thy sérvant, alle-lú-ia,   al-le-lú - ia.

Cantors

Ps. The Lórd is mý light, and my sal - vá - tion:

Choir.   *Cantors*

whóm then shall I féar? Gló-ry be.....and to

Choir

the Hó-ly Ghóst. As it wás...and év-er sh* á*ll be:

Full

wórld with-óut énd. A - men. Con - sí - der, O Lórd *(etc.)*

Alleluia   Tone VI

Cantors   *Choir*

Al - le-lú-ia.   Al - le-lú-ia.

Cantors   *Choir*

℣. Gód réign-eth óver the héa-then: Gód sítteth up-

Full

ón his hó-ly séat. Al-le-lú-ia.

Cantors — *Choir*

℣. I will not léave you cóm-fort-less: I gó awáy and cóme agáin unto you, and your héart shall re-jóice.

Full

Al - le - lú - ia.

Offertory Tone VII

Cantors

Praise the Lórd, O my sóul, while I líve will
Gód is gone úp with

I práise the Lórd: as lóng as I have ány béing
a mer - ry nóise: and the Lórd with the sóund

I will síng práises unto my Gód, al - le-lú - ia.
of the trúmp, al - le-lú - ia.

Communion Tone I

Cantors

Fá-ther, while I was with them in the wórld, I képt
thóse that thou gávest me, al - le-lú - ia:

Choir — *Cantors*

and nów I cóme to thée. I práy thee nót that thóu

Choir

shouldest táke them óut of the wórld: but that thóu shóuldest

keep them from the évil, alle-lú-ia, al-le-lú - ia.

691 WHIT-SUNDAY

Introit

Tone VII

Cantors

The Spí-rit of the Lórd hath fílled the whóle

Choir

wórld, al-le-lú-ia: and thát which contáineth

áll things hath knówledge of the vóice,

FINE

allelúia, alle-lú-ia, al-le-lú-ia.

Cantors

Ps. Let Gód aríse, and lét his é-ne-mies

Choir

be scát-ter-ed: let them álso that háte him

Cantors

flée be-fóre him. Gló-ry be.....and to the

Choir

Hó-ly Ghóst. As it wás.....and év-er shall be:

Full

wórld with-óut énd. A-men. The Spí-rit of the Lórd *(etc.)*

Alleluia   Tone II

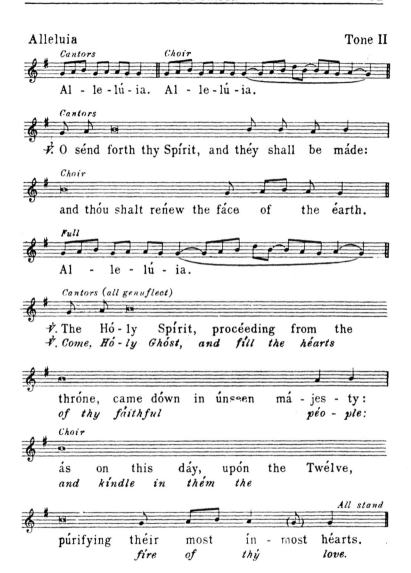

Al - le -lú - ia.   Al - le -lú - ia.

℣. O sénd forth thy Spírit, and théy shall   be   máde:

and thóu shalt reńew the fáce   of   the   éarth.

Al - le - lú - ia.

℣. The   Hó - ly   Spírit,   procéeding   from   the
℣. *Come, Hó - ly   Ghóst,   and   fíll   the   héarts*

thróne,   came dówn   in   únseen   má - jes - ty:
of   thy   fáithful   péo - ple:

ás   on   this   dáy,   upón   the   Twélve,
and   kíndle   in   thém   the

púrifying   théir   most   ín - most   héarts.
fíre   of   thý   love.

Then, without any repetition of **Alleluia** *is sung at once the following·*

WHIT-SUNDAY (continued)

Sequence   Mode I

Cóme, thou hó-ly Pá - ra-clete, And from thý ce - lés - tial séat Sénd thy líght and bríl - lian-cy. Fá-ther of the póor, draw néar; Gí-ver of all gífts, be hére; Come, the sóul's true rá - dian-cy. Come, óf cóm-fort-ers the bést, Of the sóul the swéet-est gúest, Cóme in tóil re - frésh - ing-ly: Thóu in lá-bour rést most swéet, Thóu art shá-dow from the héat, Cóm-fort in ad - vér - si - ty.

Men

O thou Light, most púre and blést, Shíne,

with - in the ín - most bréast Of thy faíth-ful

Boys

cóm - pa - ny. Whére thou árt not, mán hath nóught;

'Ev - ery hó - ly deed and thóugh Cómes from

Men

thy Di - ví - ni - ty. What is sóil - ed, make

thou púre; What is wónnd-ed, wórk its cúre;

Boys

What is párch - ed, frúc - ti - fy; What is

ríg - ed, gént -ly bénd; What is fró - zen, wárm-ly

ténd; Stréng-then what goes érr - ing - ly.

WHIT SUNDAY (continued)

Fill thy fáith - ful, who con - fíde In thy pówer to

Full

gúard and gúide, With thy séven-fold Mýs-te-ry. Hére thy

gráce and vír-tue sénd; Gránt sal - vá - tion in the énd.

And in héaven fe-lí-ci-ty. A - men, Al-le-lú-ia.

Offertory   **Tone II**

Cantors

Stá - blish the thíng, O Gód, that thóu hast

Choir

wróught in us: for thy témple's sáke at Jerúsalem,

shall kings bring présents unto thee, al - le - lú -ia.

Communion   **Tone I**

I will nót léave you cómfortless;
Súd - den - ly there cáme a sóund from

I will cóme
héaven as of a rúshing míghty wínd; and it fílled

to you yét agáin,
the whóle hóuse where they were sítting,

al - le - lú - ia: and your héart shall be
al - le - lú - ia: and they were áll filled

jóyful,
with the Hóly Ghóst and began to spéak the wónderful

alle - lú - ia al - le - lú - ia.
wórks of Gód, alle - lú - ia, al - le - lú - ia.

692 TRINITY SUNDAY
Introit Tone VII

Cantors

Bléss - ed be the Hóly Trínity, and the úndi -

Choir

-víd - ed Ú - ni - ty: we will praíse and glórify

FINE

him, becáuse he hath shéwed his mér - cy up-ón us.

Cantors *Choir*

Ps. Let us bléss the Fá-ther and the Són:
O Lórd our Gó-ver-nour: how éxcellent

Choir

with the Hó - ly Spí - rit. Glo ry be........
is thy Náme in all the wórld.

Choir

and to the Hó - ly Ghóst As it was.... and ev er

Full

shall be: world with-out end. A - men. Bless - ed be *(etc.)*

TRINITY SUNDAY (continued)

Gradual   Tone V

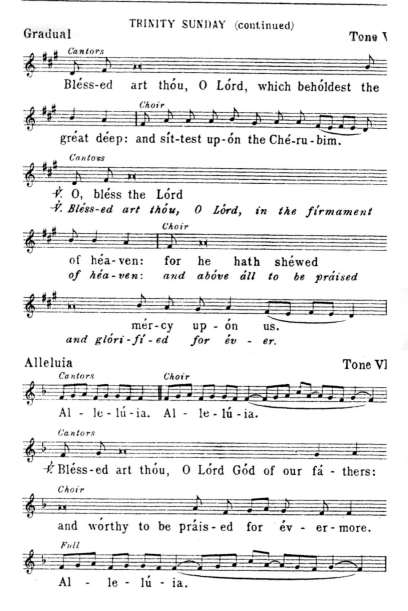

Cantors

Bléss-ed art thóu, O Lórd, which behóldest the

Choir

gréat déep: and sít-test up-ón the Ché-ru-bim.

Cantors

℣. O, bléss the Lórd
℣. *Bléss-ed art thóu, O Lórd, in the firmament*

Choir

of héa-ven: for he hath shéwed
of héa-ven: and abóve áll to be práised

mér-cy up-ón us.
and glóri-fí-ed for év - er.

Alleluia   Tone VI

Cantors   *Choir*

Al - le - lú - ia. Al - le - lú - ia.

Cantors

℣. Bléss-ed art thóu, O Lórd Gód of our fá - thers:

Choir

and wórthy to be práis-ed for év - er-more.

Full

Al - le - lú - ia.

Offertory Tone II

Cantors

Bléss-ed be Gód the Fáther, and the ónly begótten

Són of Gód; and bléssed be the Hó-ly Spi-rit:

Choir

for the mér-cy he hath dóne un-to us.

Communion Tone I

Cantors

Let us bless the God of heaven; and in the síght of

Choir

áll líving will wé give thánks un-to hím: be-cáuse

he hath dóne to ús-ward áfter his lóv-ing kínd-ness.

693 TRINITY I

Introit Tone VII

Cantors

O Lórd my Gód, in thy lóving-kíndness and

mércy have I trústed; and my héart is jóyful in

Choir

thý sal-vá-tion: I will síng unto the Lórd,

TRINITY I (continued)

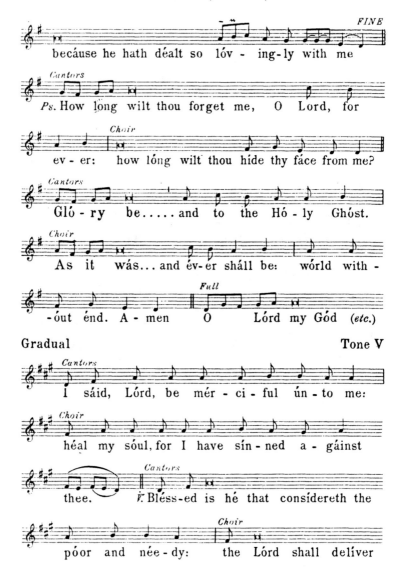

because he hath dealt so lov - ing-ly with me *FINE*

Ps. How long wilt thou forget me, O Lord, for

Choir

ev - er: how long wilt thou hide thy face from me?

Cantors

Glo - ry be..... and to the Ho - ly Ghost.

Choir

As it was... and ev-er shall be: world with -

Full

-out end. A - men   O   Lord my God (*etc.*)

Gradual   **Tone V**

Cantors

I said, Lord, be mer - ci - ful un - to me:

Choir

heal my soul, for I have sin - ned a - gainst

Cantors

thee.   ℣. Bless-ed is he that considereth the

Choir

poor and nee - dy: the Lord shall deliver

him in the time of tróu - ble.

Alleluia   Tone **VI**

Cantors   *Choir*

Al - le - lú - ia. Al - le - lú - ia.

Cantors   *Choir*

℣ Pón-der my words, O Lórd: consíder my mé-di-tá-tion.

Full

Al - le - lú - ia.

Offertory   Tone **II**

Cantors

O héar-ken thóu unto the vóice of my calling, my

Choir

Kíng and my Gód: for ún-to thée will I máke my práyer.

Communion   Tone **I**

Cantors

I will spéak of áll thy márvellous wórks; I

Choir

will be glád, and re-jóice in thee: yéa, my

Choir

sóngs will I máke of thy Náme, O most Hígh-est.

694　　　　　　　TRINITY II

Introit　　　　　　　　　　　　　　　　Tone VII

Cantors
The Lórd was my réfuge and my uphólder;

and he bróught me fórth into a pláce of lí-

Choir
-ber - ty: he de - lívered me, becáuse

FINE
he de - líght - ed in me.

Cantors
Ps. I will lóve thee, O Lórd my stréngth:

Choir
the Lórd is my róck, my fór-tress and my Sá-viour

Cantors
Gló - ry be...... and to the Hó ly Ghóst.

Choir
As it was..... and év-er shall bé: wórld with-

Full
-óut end. A - men. The Lórd was my réfuge (*etc.*)

Gradual Tone V

Cantors

Whén I was in tróuble I cáll-ed up-ón the Lórd:

Choir

and he héard me.

Cantors

℣. De-lí-ver my sóul, O Lórd,

Choir

from lý-ing lips: and fróm a de-céit-ful tóngue.

Alleluia Tone VI

Cantors   *Choir*

Al - le - lú - ia.   Al - le - lú - ia.

Cantors

℣. God is a rightéous Júdge, stróng and pá - tient:
℣. *O Lórd my Gód, in thée have I pút my trúst:*

Choir

and Gód is pro - - vók -
sáve me from áll them that pérsecute me, and

Full.

-ed év - ery day. Al - le - lu - ia
de - lí - ver me.

Offertory Tone II

Cantors

Túrn thee, O Lórd, and de - lí - ver my sóul:

Choir

O sáve me for thy mér - cies' sáke.

TRINITY II (continued)

Communion   Tone I

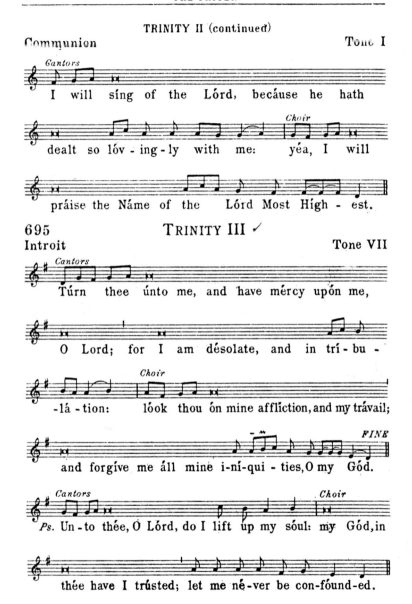

I will síng of the Lórd, becáuse he hath dealt so lóv - ing - ly with me: yéa, I will práise the Náme of the Lórd Most Hígh - est.

695   TRINITY III ✓

Introit   Tone VII

Túrn thee únto me, and have mércy upón me, O Lord; for I am désolate, and in trí - bu - -lá - tion: lóok thou ón mine afflíction, and my trávail; and forgíve me áll mine i-ní-qui - ties, O my Gód. *FINE*

Ps. Un -to thée, O Lórd, do I lift úp my sóul: my Gód, in thée have I trústed; let me né-ver be con-fóund-ed.

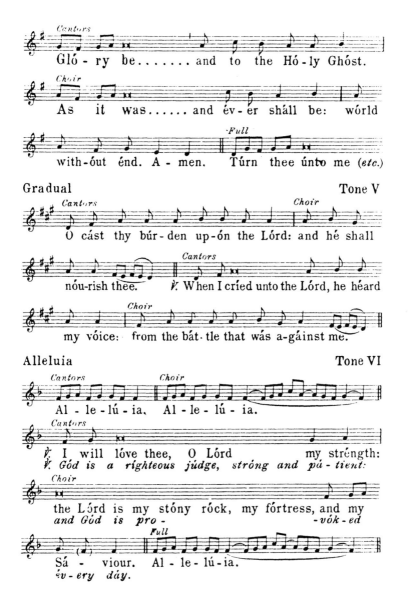

Gló - ry be . . . . and to the Hó - ly Ghóst.

As it was . . . . . . and év - er shall be: world

with-óut énd. A - men. Túrn thee únto me (*etc.*)

Gradual   Tone V

O cást thy búr - den up-ón the Lórd: and hé shall

nóu-rish thee. ℣. When I cried unto the Lórd, he héard

my vóice: from the bát· tle that wás a-gáinst me.

Alleluia   Tone VI

Al - le - lú - ia, Al - le - lú - ia.

℣. I will lóve thee, O Lórd my stréngth:
℣. *Gód is a ríghteous júdge, stróng and pá - tient:*

the Lórd is my stóny róck, my fórtress, and my
and Gód is pro -   - vók - ed

Sá - viour. Al - le - lú - ia.
év - ery dáy.

TRINITY III (continued)

Offertory   Tone II

Cantors

Théy that knów thy Náme will put their trúst in thee;

for thóu, Lórd, hast néver fáil-ed thém that séek thee:

Choir

O práise the Lórd which dwélleth in Sýon; for he

forgétteth nót the com-pláint of the póor.

Communion.   Tone I

Cantors

I have cálled upon thée, O Gód, for
I say unto yóu, There is jóy in the présence of the

Choir

thóu shalt héar me: in - clíne thine éar unto
Án - gels of Gód: *ó - ver óne*

me, and héar - ken ún - to my   words.
sín - ner that re - pént - eth.

696   TRINITY IV

Introit   Tone VII

Cantors

The Lórd is my líght, and my sálvation,

whom thén shall I féar? the Lórd is the strónghold

of my life, of whom shall I be a - fraid?

Choir

when mine enemies pressed sore against me,

FINE *Cantors*

they stum - bled and fell. *Ps.* Though an

Choir

host of men were laid a-gainst me: yet shall not my

Cantors

heart be a - fraid. Glo - ry be...... and to the

Choir

Ho-ly Ghost. As it was.... and év-er shall be:

Full

world with - out end. A - men. The Lord is my light (*etc.*)

Gradual   Tone V

Cantors

Be mer - ciful, O Lord, un - to our sins:

Choir

where - fore do the heathen say, Where is

Cantors

now their God? ℣. Help us, O God of our

TRINITY IV (continued)

Choir

sal - vá - tion: and for the hónour of thy

Náme, de - lí - ver us, O Lórd.

Alleluia   Tone VI

Cantors   *Choir*

Al - le - lú - ia. Al - le - lú - ia.

Cantors

℣ The Kíng shall rejóice in thy
℣ *Thóu, O Gód, art sét in the thróne that*

Choir

stréngth, O Lórd: excéeding glád shall he bé
júdg - est right: be thóu the réfuge of the

of thý sal - vá - tion.
opprést in due tíme of tróu - ble.

Full

Al - le - lú - ia.

Offertory   Tone II

Cantors

Líght - en mine éyes, that I sléep not

Choir

in déath; lest mine énemy sáy,

I have pre - váil - ed a - gáinst him.

Communion   Tone I

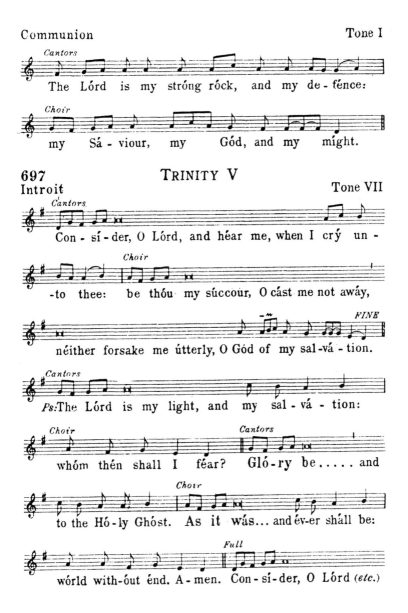

Cantors

The Lórd is my stróng róck, and my de-fénce:

Choir

my Sá-viour, my Gód, and my míght.

697   TRINITY V

Introit   Tone VII

Cantors

Con-sí-der, O Lórd, and héar me, when I crý un-

Choir

-to thee: be thóu my súccoúr, O cást me not awáy,

FINE

néither forsake me útterly, O Gód of my sal-vá-tion.

Cantors

Ps: The Lórd is my light, and my sal-vá-tion:

Choir   *Cantors*

whóm thén shall I féar? Gló-ry be..... and

Choir

to the Hó-ly Ghóst. As it wás... and év-er shàll be:

Full

wórld with-óut énd. A-men. Con-sí-der, O Lórd *(etc.)*

Gradual   TRINITY V (continued)   Tone V

Be - hóld, O Gód, our de - fénd - er: and lóok

up - ón thy sér - vants.   ℣. O Lórd Gód

of hósts: hear the práyers of thy sér - vants.

Alleluia   Tone VI

Al - le - lú - ia. Al - le - lú - ia.

℣ In thée, O Lórd, have I pút my trúst,
℣ *The King shall rejóice in thy stréngth,*

let me néver be put to con - fú - sion:
                                O Lórd:

rid me and delíver me in thy ríghteousness,
excéeding glád shall he bé of

bow dówn thine éar to me, make háste to hélp me.
                        thý sal - vá - tion.

Al - le - lú - ia.

Offertory

Tone II

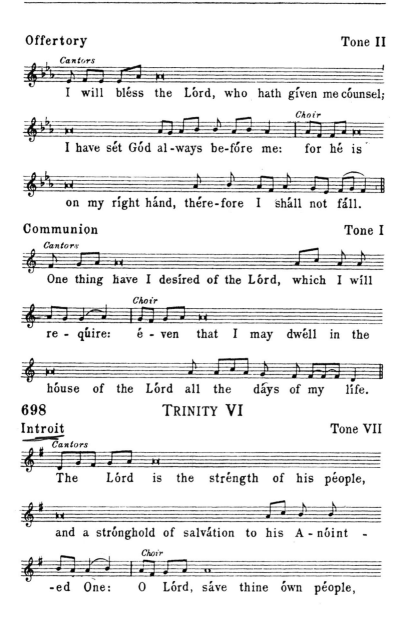

Cantors

I will bléss the Lórd, who hath gíven me cóunsel;

I have sét Gód al -ways be-fóre me: for hé is

on my ríght hánd, thére-fore I sháll not fáll.

Communion

Tone I

Cantors

One thing have I desíred of the Lórd, which I wíll

Choir

re - qúire: é - ven that I may dwéll in the

hóuse of the Lórd all the dáys of my lífe.

698

TRINITY VI

Introit

Tone VII

Cantors

The Lórd is the stréngth of his péople,

and a strónghold of salvátion to his A - nóint -

Choir

-ed One: O Lórd, sáve thine ówn péople,

TRINITY VI (continued)

and gíve thy bléssing unto thíne inhéritance;

O féed them álso, and sét them úp

for év - er. *Ps.* Un - to thée will I

crý, O Lórd; my Gód, be not sí -

-lent ún - to me: lést, if thou make as though

thou héarest nót, I becóme líke thém that go

dówn in - to the pít. Gló - ry be.... and to

the Hó - ly Ghóst As it wás.... and év - er

sháll be wórld with - óut énd. A - men.

The Lórd is the stréngth of his péople (*etc.*)

Gradual   Tone V

Túrn thee a - gáin, O Lórd, at the lást:

and be grá - cious ún - to thy sér - vants.

℣. Lórd, thou hast béen our ré - fuge: from

óne generátion to an - ó - ther.

Alleluia   Tone VI

Al - le - lú - ia. Al - le - lú - ia.

℣. O de - líver me from mine énemies,
℣. *In thée, O Lórd, have I pút my trúst,*

O Gód:

let me néver pút to con - fú - sion:

defénd me from thém that ríse
delíver me in thy ríghteousness; bow dówn

úp a - gáinst me.
thine éar to mé, make háste to de - lí - ver me.

Al - le - lú - ia.

TRINITY VI (continued)

Offertory   Tone II

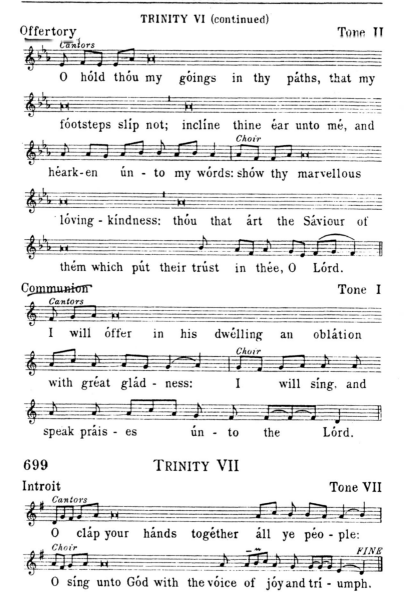

Cantors

O hóld thóu my góings in thy páths, that my

fóotsteps slíp not; inclíne thine éar unto mé, and

Choir

héark-en ún - to my wórds: shów thy marvellous

lóving - kíndness: thóu that árt the Sáviour of

thém which pút their trúst in thée, O Lórd.

Communion   Tone I

Cantors

I will óffer in his dwélling an oblátion

Choir

with gréat glád - ness: I will síng, and

speak práis - es ún - to the Lórd.

699   TRINITY VII

Introit   Tone VII

Cantors

O cláp your hánds togéther áll ye péo - ple:

Choir   *FINE*

O síng unto Gód with the vóice of jóy and trí - umph.

Ps. Hé shall subdúe the péo-ple ún-der us:
Ps. Fór the Lórd is hígh, and to be féar - ed:

and the nátions ún - der óur féet.
he is the gréat Kíng up - on áll the éarth.

Glo - ry be... and to the Hó - ly Ghóst. As it

was... and év - er shǎll be: wórld with - óut énd.

A - men. O cláp your hánds togéther *(etc.)*

Gradual   Tone V

Cóme, ye children, and héark - en ún - to me:

I will téach you the féar of the Lórd.

℣ Cóme un - to mé and be en - light -
℣ Théy had an éye unto hím, and wére en - light -

-en - ed: and your fáces shall nót be a - shám-ed.
- en - ed: and their fáces were not a - shám-ed:

TRINITY VII (continued)

Alleluia Tone VI

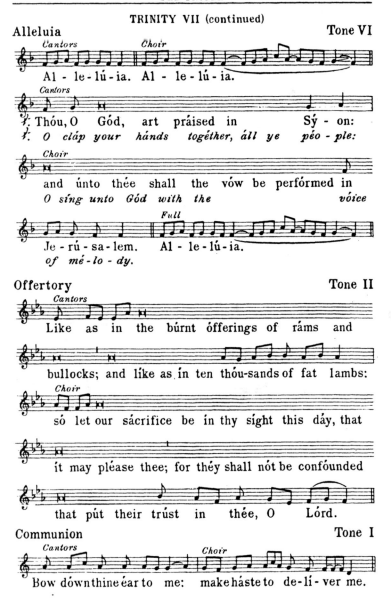

Cantors ... *Choir*

Al - le - lú - ia. Al - le - lú - ia.

Cantors

℣. Thóu, O God, art práised in Sý - on:
℣. *O cláp your hánds togéther, áll ye péo - ple:*

Choir

and únto thée shall the vów be perfórmed in
O síng unto Gód with the vóice

Full

Je - rú - sa - lem. Al - le - lú - ia.
of mé - lo - dy.

Offertory Tone II

Cantors

Like as in the búrnt ófferings of ráms and

bullocks; and líke as ín ten thóu-sands of fat lambs:

Choir

só let our sácrifice be ín thy síght this dáy, that

ít may pléase thee; for théy shall nót be confóunded

that pút their trúst in thée, O Lórd.

Communion Tone I

Cantors ... *Choir*

Bow dównthine éar to me: make háste to de-lí - ver me.

700   TRINITY VIII ✓

Introit   Tone VII

Cantors

We háve wáited, O Gód, for thy lóving-kíndness

in the mídst of thy témple; accórding to thy Náme,

O Gód, só is thy práise ún - to the wórld's énd:

Choir   *FINE*

thy ríght hand is fúll   of rígh - teous - ness.

Cantors

Ps. Gréat is   the Lórd, and high - ly to be práis - ed:

Choir

in the cíty of our Gód, even up - ón his hó - ly híll.

Cantors   *Choir*

Glo-ry be... and to the Hó-ly Ghóst. As it   was... and

Full

év-er sháll be: wórld with-óut énd. A-men. We have wáited
                                                    (etc.)

Gradual   Tone V

Cantors

Be thóu my strong róck, and hóuse of de-fénce:

Choir   *Cantors*

that thou may-est save me.   ℣. In thée, O Lórd,

TRINITY VIII (continued)

have I pút my trúst: let me néver be pút to con-fú - sion.

Alleluia   **Tone VI**

Cantors   *Choir*

Al - le - lú - ia.   Al - le - lú - ia.

Cantors

℣. Héar   my   law:
℣. Gréat   is   the   Lord, and   híghly   to   be   práis - ed:

Choir

O my
in   the   cíty   of   our   God,   even   up - on his

Full

peo - ple.   Al - le - lú - ia.
ho - ly   hill.

Offertory   **Tone II**

Cantors

Thóu shalt sáve the péople that are ín advérsity,

O Lórd, and shalt bríng down the hígh lóoks of the próud:

Choir

for   whó   is   Gód,   but   the   Lórd?

Communion   **Tone I**

Cantors

O   táste   and see how grá - cious the Lórd   is:

Choir

bléss - ed is hé that pút - teth his trúst in   hím.

701 TRINITY IX

Introit Tone VII

Cantors

Be - hóld, God is my hélper; the Lórd is he that up -

Choir

-hóld - eth my sóul: re - wárd

thou évil unto mine énemies; destróy them

in thine ánger, for thy ríghteousness sáke,

FINE

O Lórd my stréngth and my de - fénd - er.

Cantors

Ps. Sáve me, O Gód, for thy Náme's sáke:

Choir *Cantors*

and a - vénge me in thý stréngth. Glo - ry be...

Choir

and to the Hó - ly Ghóst. As it was... and

év - er sháll be: wórld with - óut énd. A - men.

Full

Be - hóld, Gód is my hélper *(etc.)*

TRINITY IX   continued

Gradual   Tone V

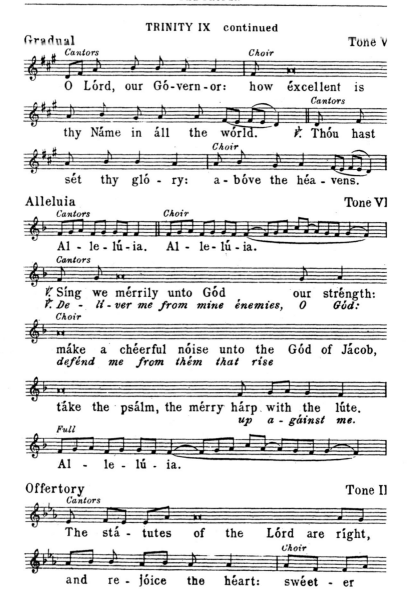

Cantors   *Choir*

O Lórd, our Gó-vern-or: how éxcellent is

Cantors

thy Náme in áll the world. ℣. Thóu hast

Choir

sét thy gló - ry: a - bóve the héa - vens.

Alleluia   Tone VI

Cantors   *Choir*

Al - le - lú - ia.   Al - le - lú - ia.

Cantors

℣. Síng we mérrily unto Gód   our stréngth:
℣. *De - lí - ver me from mine énemies, O   Gód:*

Choir

máke a chéerful nóise unto the Gód of Jácob,
defénd me from thém that ríse

táke the psálm, the mérry hárp with the lúte.
                   up a - gáinst me.

Full

Al - le - lú - ia.

Offertory   Tone II

Cantors

The stá - tutes of the Lórd are ríght,

Choir

and re - jóice the héart: swéet - er

also than hóney, and the hóney - comb;

moreóver, by them is thy sér - vant táught.

Communion Tone I

Cantors

Séek ye fírst of áll the kíng - dom
Hé that éateth my Flésh, and drínk - eth

Choir

of Gód: and áll these thíngs shall be
my Blóod: dwéll - eth in

ádded un - to you, sáith the Lórd.
mé, and I in hím.

702 TRINITY X

Introit Tone VII

Cantors

When I cálled upón the♦ Lórd, he regárded

my petítion; yéa, from the báttle that was a-gáinst me:

Choir

and he hath bróught them dówn, éven hé that ís

of óld, and endúreth for éver; O cást thy búrden

FINE

upon the Lórd, and hé shall nóu - rish theє.

TRINITY X (continued)

Cantors

Ps. Héar my práyer, O Lórd, and híde not
thy - sélf from mý pe-tí-tion: take héed un - to

Choir

Cantors

mé, and héar me. Gló-ry be........ and tó the
Hó - ly Ghóst. As it wás..... and év-er sh* ll be:

Choir

Full

wórld with-óut énd A - men. When I cálled (*etc.*)

Gradual   Tone V

Cantors

Kéep me, O Lórd, as the áp-ple of an éye:

Choir

híde me ún - der the shá-dow of thy wíngs.

Cantors

℣. Let my sén-tence come fórth from thy pré-sence:

Choir

and lét thine éyes lóok upon the thíng that is é-quál.

Alleluia   Tone VI

Cantors   *Choir*

Al - le - lú - ia.   Al - le - lú - ia.

Cantors

℣. O   Lórd   Gód   of   my   sal-   vá - tion:
℣. *Thóu,   O   Gód,   art   práised   in   Sý - on:*

Choir

I have cried dáy and   níght be -
and únto thée shall the vow be perfórmed in   Je -

Full

-fóre   thee.   Al - le - lú - ia.
-rú - sa - lem

Offertory   Tone II

Cantors

Un - to thée, O Lórd, líft I úp my sóul; O my Gód,

in thée have I trústed, let me nót be con-fóund-ed:

Choir

néi - ther let mine énemies tríumph óver me; for áll

théy that hópe for thée shall nót be a-shám-ed.

Communion   Tone I

Cantors

Thóu shalt be pléased with the sá - cri - fice

Choir

of rígh - teous - ness: with the búrnt ófferings

and oblátions upón thine ál - tar, O   Lórd.

703   TRINITY XI

Introit   Tone VII

Cantors
Gód in his hóly habitátion, it is hé

that máketh bréthren to be of óne mínd

in an hóuse: hé will gíve the domínion

and pre - éminence ún - to his péo - ple. *FINE*

Cantors
Ps. Let Gód aríse, and lét his é - ne - mies

be scát-ter ed: lét them álso that háte him

fleé be - fóre him *Cantors* Gló - ry be...... and to the

Choir Hó - ly Ghóst. As it wás..... and év - er

sháll be: wórld with-óut énd. A - men.

Full
Gód in his hóly habitátion. *(etc.)*

Gradual Tone V

Cantors
My héart hath trústed in Gód, and Í am

Choir
hélp - ed: thére - fore my héart dánceth for jóy, and

ín my sóng will I práise him.

Cantors *Choir*
℣. Un - to thée will I crý, O Lórd: be not sílent,

O my Gód, nor de - párt from me

Alleluia Tone VI

Cantors *Choir*
Al - le - lú - ia. Al - le - lú - ia.

Cantors
℣. Lórd, thou hast béen our
℣. *Sing we mérrily unto Gód our stréngth; make a*

ré - fuge:
chéerful nóise unto the Gód of Já - cob:

Choir
from óne generátion to a - nó - ther.
táke the psalm, bring hí - ther the tá - bret.

Full
Al - le - lú - ia.

TRINITY XI (continued)

Offertory   Tone II

I will mág-nify thée, O Lórd, for thóu hast

Choir

sét me úp: and nót made my fóes to trí-umph

Cantors

ó - ver me.   O Lórd, my Gód, I crí - ed

Choir

ún - to thee: and thóu hast héal-ed me.

Communion   Tone I

Cantors

Hó - nour the Lórd with thy súbstance,

and with the fírst - fruits of áll thine ín - crease:

Choir

só shall thy bárns be fílled with plénty,

and thy présses shall burst óut with néw wíne.

704   TRINITY XII

Introit   Tone VII

Cantors

Háste thee, O Gód, únto my réscue, and sáve me;

O Lórd, make háste to mý de - lí - ver - ance:

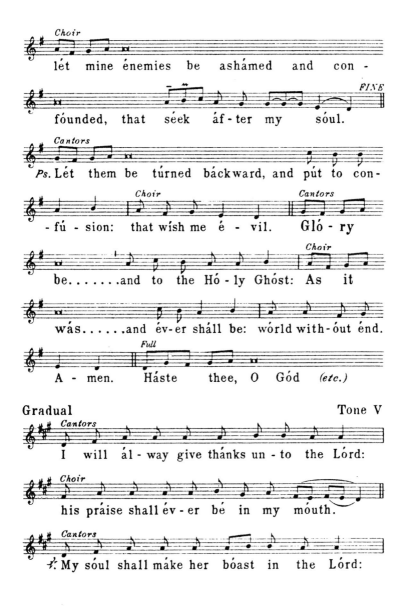

Choir
lét mine énemies be ashámed and con -

FINE
fóunded, that séek áf - ter my sóul.

Cantors
Ps. Lét them be túrned báckward, and pút to con-

Choir
- fú - sion: that wísh me é - vil.

Cantors
Gló - ry

be.......and to the Hó - ly Ghóst: As it

Choir
wás......and év - er shȧll be: wórld with - óut énd.

Full
A - men. Háste thee, O Gód *(etc.)*

Gradual   Tone V

Cantors
I will ál - way give thánks un - to the Lórd:

Choir
his práise shall év - er bé in my móuth.

Cantors
℣. My sóul shall máke her bóast in the Lórd:

TRINITY XII (continued)

the húmble shall héar there-óf, and be glád.

Alleluia   **Tone VI**

Cantors   *Choir*

Al - le - lu - ia.   Al - le - lu - ia.

Cantors

℣. O cóme,   let   us   síng   únto   the   Lórd:
℣. *O Lórd   Gód   of   mý   sal - vá - tion:*

Choir

lét us héartily   rejóice   in   the   stréngth   of   óur
I have   críed   dáy   and   níght

Full

sal-vá-tion. Al - le - lú - ia.
be-fóre thee.

Offertory   **Tone II**

Cantors

Mó - ses   be - sóught   the   Lórd   his   Gód

Choir

and sáid: Whý,   O   Lórd,   doth   thy   wráth   wax

Cantors

hót a - gáinst   thy   péo-ple?   Túrn   from   thy   fíerce

wráth; remémber   Ábraham,   Ís - aac,   and   Já - cob:

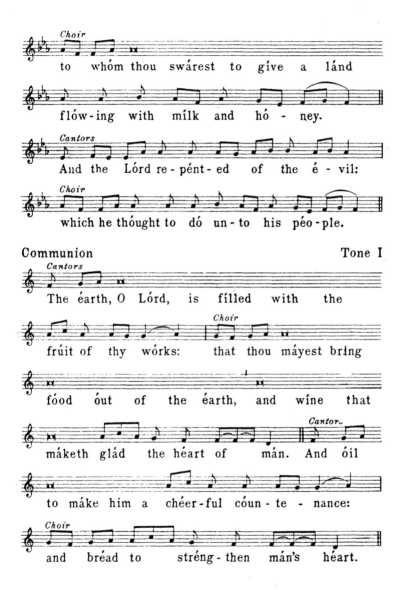

Choir

to whóm thou swárest to gíve a lánd

flów-ing with mílk and hó - ney.

Cantors

And the Lórd re - pént - ed of the é - vil:

Choir

which he thóught to dó un - to his péo - ple.

Communion   Tone I

Cantors

The éarth, O Lórd, is fílled with the

Choir

frúit of thy wórks: that thou máyest bring

fóod óut of the éarth, and wíne that

Cantor

máketh glád the héart of mán. And óil

to máke him a chéer - ful cóun - te - nance:

Choir

and bréad to stréng - then mán's héart.

705   TRINITY XIII

Introit   Tono VII

Cantors

Lóok, O Lórd, gráciously upón thy cóvenant,

and forsáke not the cóngregátion of the

Choir

póor for év - er: a - ríse, O Lórd, maintáin

thine ówn cáuse; and bé not unmíndful of the

FINE

vói - ces of thém that séek thee.

Cantors

Ps. O Gód, whérefore árt thou ábsent fróm us

Choir

so lóng: whý is thy wráth so hót agáinst the

Cantors

shéep of thy pás - ture? Gló - ry be..... and to the

Choir

Hó - ly Ghóst. As it wás.... and év - er shall be:

Full

wórld with-óut énd. A - men. Lóok, O Lórd *(etc.)*

Gradual Tone V

Cantors

Look up - ón thy có - ve - nant, O Lórd:

Choir

and forgét not the cóngregátion of the

póor for év - er. ℣. A - ríse, O Lórd, main-

-táin thine ówn cáuse: re - mémber hów the fóolish

mán blas - phém - eth thee dái - ly.

Alleluia Tone VI

Cantors *Choir*

Al - le - lú - ia. Al - le - lú - ia.

Cantors *Choir*

℣. For the Lórd is a gréat Gód: and a gréat Kíng
℣. *Lórd, thou hast béen our ré - fuge*: *from óne generátion*

Full

ó - ver áll the éarth. Al - le - lú - ia.
to a - no - ther.

Offertory Tone II

Cantors *Choir*

My hópe hath béen in thée, O Lórd: I have sáid,

Thóu art my Gód, my tíme is ín thy hánd.

TRINITY XIII (continued)

Communion   Tone I

Cantors

Thóu hast gíven us Bréad from héa-ven, O   Lórd:

Choir

háv-ing évery delíght, and év-ery táste of swéet-ness.

706   TRINITY XIV
Introit   Tone VII

Cantors

Be - hóld, O Gód, our défender, and lóok upon

Choir

the fáce of thíne A - nóint-ed: for óne dáy in

FINE

thy cóurts is bét-ter   than a thóu - sand.

Cantors

Ps. O   how ámiable are thy dwéll ings, thou Lórd of hósts:

Choir

my sóul hath a   desíre and lónging to énter

Cantors

into the cóurts of the Lórd.   Gló-ry   be..... and to

Choir

the Hó-ly Ghóst.   As it   wás..... and év-er shall be

Full

wórld with óut énd. A - men.   Be - hóld, O Gód (*etc.*)

Gradual   Tone V

Cantors

It is a good thing to give thanks un - to
Is is better to trust in

Choir

the Lord: and to sing praises unto thy
the Lord: than to put any

Cantors

Name, O most High - est. ℣. To tell
cón - fi - dence in mán. ℣. It is

of thy loving-kindness early in the morn - ing:
better to trust in the Lord:

Choir

and of thy truth in the night sea - son.
than to put any cónfi-dence in prin - ces.

Alleluia   Tone VI

Cantors   Choir

Al - le - lú - ia. Al - le - lú - ia.

Cantors

℣. O give thanks unto the Lord, and call upon
℣. O cóme, let us sing únto

Choir

his Name: tell the people what
the Lord: lét us heartily rejóice in the stréngth of

Full

things he hath done. Al - le - lú - ia.
óur sal - vá - tion.

TRINITY XIV (continued)

Offertory   Tone II

Cantors

The Án-gel of the Lórd tárrieth róund about

thém that féar him, and de - lí - ver - eth them:

Choir

O táste and sée how grá-cious the Lórd is.

Communion   Tone I

Cantors   *Choir*

The Bréad that I will give is my flésh: which I
Séek ye first the kíng-dom of Gód: and áll

will give for the lífe of the wórld.
these things shall be ádded un-to yóu, sáith the Lórd.

707   TRINITY XV

Introit   Tone VII

Cantors

Bów dówn, O Lórd, thine éar to me, and

Choir

héar me: O my Gód, sáve thy sérvant that

trústeth in thée; have mércy upón me, O Lórd,

FINE

for I have cálled dái - ly up-ón thee.

Ps. Cóm - fort the sóul of thy sér - vant:

for únto thée, O Lórd, do I líft up my sóul.

Gló - ry be..... and tó the Hó - ly Ghóst.

As it wás..... év - er shǎll be: wórld with -

-óut énd. A - men. Bów dówn, O Lórd *(etc.)*

Gradual   Tone V

It is bétter to trúst_____ in
It is a góod thíng to give thánks un - to

the Lórd: than to pút any cón - fi -
the Lórd: and to síng práises únto thy Náme, O

-dence in mán. ℣. It is bétter to
most Hígh - est. ℣. To téll of thy lóving -

trúst_____ in the Lórd:
-kíndness éarly, in the mórn - ing:

than to pút any cónfi - dence in prín - ces.
and of thy trúth in the níght séa - son.

TRINITY XV (continued)

Alleluia   Tone VI

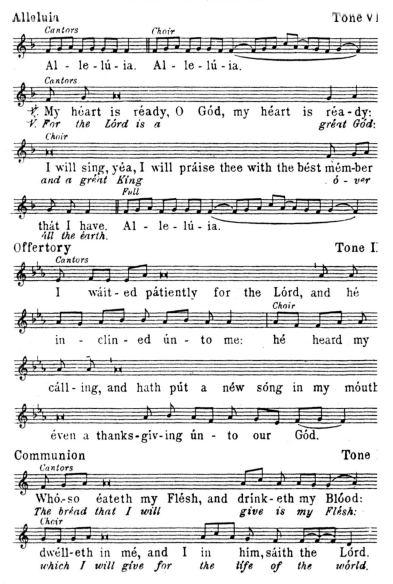

Cantors   *Choir*

Al - le - lú - ia.   Al - le - lú - ia.

Cantors

℣. My héart is réady, O God, my héart is réa - dy:
℣. *For the Lórd is a gréat Gód:*

Choir

I will sing, yéa, I will práise thee with the bést mém-ber
and a gréat Kíng . ó - ver

Full

thát I have.   Al - le - lú - ia.
áll the éarth.

Offertory   Tone II

Cantors

I wáit - ed pátiently for the Lórd, and hé

Choir

in - clín - ed ún - to me: hé heard my

cáll - ing, and hath pút a néw sóng in my móuth

éven a thanks-gív-ing ún - to our Gód.

Communion   Tone

Cantors

Whó-so éateth my Flésh, and drínk-eth my Blóod:
The bréad that I will give is my Flésh:

Choir

dwéll-eth in mé, and I in him, sáith the Lórd.
which I will gíve for the lífe of the wórld.

708

Trinity XVI

Introit   Tone VII

Cantors

Have mér-cy upón me, O Lórd, for I have
called dái-ly up-ón thee:

Choir

for thóu, O Lórd, art
grácious and mérciful, and plénteous in thy lóving-kindness
toward áll thém that cáll up-on thee.

FINE

Cantors

Ps. Bow dówn thine éar, O Lórd, and héar me:

Choir for I am póor and in mí-se-ry.

Cantors Gló-ry be ....
and to the Hó-ly Ghóst. As it wás....and év-er sháll be:

Choir

Full

wórld with-out énd. A-men. Have mér-cy upón me *(etc.)*

Gradual   Tone V

Cantors

The héa-then shall féar thy Náme, O Lórd:

Choir

and áll the kings of the éarth thy má-jes-ty.

TRINITY XVI (continued)

Cantors

℣. Whén the Lórd shall búild up Sý - on:

Choir

and whén his gló - ry sháll ap - pear.

Alleluia   **Tone VI**

Cantors   *Choir*

Al - le - lú - ia. Al - le - lú - ia.

Cantors

℣. Ye that féar the Lórd, pút your trúst in the Lórd:
℣. O sing unto the Lórd a néw sóng:

Choir

hé is their hélper, and de - fénd - er.
for hé hath done már - vel - lous things.

Full

Al - le - lú - ia.

Offertory   **Tone II**

Cantors

Look dówn, O Lórd, to hélp me;

lét them be ashámed, and confoúnded togéther, that

séek áfter my soúl to de - stróy it:

Choir

look dówn, O Lórd, to hélp me.

Communion Tone I

Cantors

O Lórd, I will máke méntion of thy

ríghteousness ónly; thóu. Gód, hast taúght me from my

Choir

yóuth úp un - til nów: for - sáke me nót, O Gód,

in my óld áge, when I am gráy - héad - ed.

709

TRINITY XVII

Introit Tone VII

Cantors

Rígh - teous art thóu, O Lórd, and trúe is thy júdge-ment:

Choir

déal with thy sérvant accórding únto thy mér - ci - ful

FINE Cantors

kind - ness. *Ps.* Bléss-ed are thóse that are ún - de - fí - led

Choir *Cantors*

in the wáy: and wálk in the láw of the Lórd. Gló - ry be ....

Choir

and tó the Hó - ly Ghóst. As it wás .... and év-er sháll be

Full

wórld with - óut énd. **A** - men. Rígh - teous art thóu *(etc.)*

TRINITY XVII (continued)

Gradual　　　　　　　　　　　　　　　　　　Tone V

Cantors

Bléss-ed is the péople whose Gód is the Lórd:

Choir

and bléssed are the fólk that he hath chósen

to him to be his in-hé-ri-tance.

Cantors

℣. By the Wórd of the Lórd were the héa-vens máde

Choir

and áll the hósts of thém by the bréath of his móuth.

Alleluia　　　　　　　　　　　　　　　　　　Tone VI

Cantors　　　　　　　*Choir*

Al - le - lú - ia. Al - le - lú - ia

Cantors

℣. The right hánd of the Lórd bringeth míghty things to páss
℣. *Héar my*　　　　　　　　　　　　　*práyer, O Lórd*

Choir

the right hánd of the Lórd háth the pre-ém-in-ence.
and lét my crý　　　　　　*cóme un-to thée.*

Full

Al - le - lú - ia.

Offertory
Tone II

Cantors

I, Dán - iel, práy - ed un - to the Lórd

Choir

my Gód, and sáid: Héar, O our Gód, the práyer of

Cantors

thy sér - vant. Cáuse thy fáce to shíne upón thy

Choir

sánc - tu - a - ry: and be - hóld, O Gód, this

thy peóple, who are cáll - ed by thy Náme.

Communion
Tone I

Cantors

Pró - mise unto the Lórd your Gód, and kéep it:

Choir

all yé that are róund abóut him bring présents

Cantors

unto hím that óught to be feár - ed. Hé shall

Choir

re - fráin the spí - rit of prín - ces: and is

wónderful a - móng the kíngs of the éarth.

710 TRINITY XVIII

Introit   Tone VII

Cantors

Give péace, O Lórd, to thém that wáit for thee,

and lét thy Próphets be fóund fáith-ful:

Choir

re - gárd the práyers of thy sérvant, and of thy

péo - ple Ís - ra - el. *Ps.* I was glád when they *FINE* *Cantors*

Choir

sáid un-to mé: we will gó into the hóuse of the Lórd.

Cantors

Gló - ry be .... and tó the Hó - ly Ghóst.

Choir

As it wás... and év- er sháll be: wórld with-

Full

-óut énd. A - men. Give péace, O Lórd, *(etc.)*

Gradual   Tone V

Cantors

I was glád when they sáid un - to me:

Choir

we will gó into the hóuse of the Lórd.

℣. Peace be with-in thy walls: and plenteousness within thy pa-la-ces.

Alleluia   **Tone VI**

Al-le-lú-ia. Al-le-lú-ia.

℣. I was glád when they sáid un-to mé:
℣. *The héa-then shall féar thy Náme, O Lord:*

we will gó into the hóuse of the Lórd.
and áll the kíngs of the éarth thy má-jes-ty.

Al-le-lú-ia.

Offertory   **Tone II**

Mó-ses cón-secrated an áltar unto the Lórd, óffering búrnt ófferings upón it, and sá-cri-fi-cing péace óf-fer-ings:

and he máde an évening sácrifice for a

TRINITY XVIII (continued)

sweet - smélling sávour únto the Lórd Gód,

in the síght of the chíl-dren of 'Is - ra - el.

Communion   **Tone I**
Cantors

Bring óf - ferings, and cóme ín - to his cóurts:

Choir

O wór-ship the Lórd in the béau-ty of hó - li - ness.

711   TRINITY XIX

Introit   **Tone VII**
Cantors

I am the sáving héalth of my péople, sáith

Choir

the Lórd Gód: óut of whátsoéver tribulátion

they shall práy to me, I will súrely hélp them,

FINE

and I will bé their Gód for év - er and év - er.

Cantors   *Choir*

Ps. Héar my láw, O my péo - ple: inclíne your éars

Cantors

unto the wórds of mý móuth   Gló- ry   be .... and

Choir

tó the Hó-ly Ghóst.   As it wás... and év-er shǎll be:

Full

wórld withóut énd. A-men.   I   am the sáving héalth(*etc.*)

Gradual   Tone V

Cantors

Lét   my práyer   be   sét   forth   ín   thy   síght:

Choir   Cantors

O Lórd, as the in - cénse: ℞. And lét the líft-ing

Choir

úp of mý hánds: be an éve-ning sa-cri - fice.

Alleluia   Tone VI

Cantors   Choir

Al - le - lú - ia.   Al - le - lú - ia.

Cantors

℞. Théy that pút their trúst in the Lórd shall be éven as
℞. *O give thánks unto the Lórd, and cáll upon*

Choir

the móunt Sý - on: hé who dwélleth in Jerúsalem
his Náme: téll   the péople what

may nót be remóved, but stándeth fást for   év - er.
things he hath done.

Full

Al - le - lú - ia.

TRINITY XIX (continued)

Offertory   Tone II

Cantors
Though I walk in the midst of trouble, yet shalt

Choir
thou re - fresh me, O Lord: thou shalt stretch forth

thy right hand upon the furiousness of mine enemies,

and thy right hand shall save me.

Communion   Tone I

Cantors
Thou hast charged that we shall diligently

Choir
keep thy com-mand-ments: 'O that my ways were made

so direct, that 'I might keep thy sta - tutes.

712   TRINITY XX

Introit   Tone VII

Cantors
Ev - ery - thing that thou hast brought upon

us, O Lord God, thou hast done in righ-teous-ness

and júdge-ment: for wé have tréspassed agáinst

thee, and have not obéyed thy commándments;

but give glórv and hónour to thý Náme,

and déal with us accórding to the

múltitude of thy tén - der mér - cies.

Ps. Gréat is the Lórd, and híghly to be práis - ed:
Ps. Bléss-ed are thóse that are únde-fíl-ed in the wáy:

in the cíty of our Gód, éven up-ón his hó-ly híll.
and wálk in the láw of the Lórd.

Gló - ry be.... and tó the Hó - ly Ghóst.

As it wás... and év-er shall be: wórld with-

-óut end. A - men. 'Ev - ery - thing *(etc.)*

Gradual   TRINITY XX (continued)   Tone V

Cantors
The éyes of áll wáit up-on thée, O Lórd:

Choir
and thou gívest them their méat in due séa-son.

Cantors
℣ Thou ó-pen-est thy hánd: *Choir* and fíllest

áll things lív-ing with plén-teous-ness.

Alleluia   Tone VI

Cantors   *Choir*
Al - le - lú-ia.   Al - le - lú - ia.

Cantors
℣ Out of the déep have I cálled unto thée, O Lórd:
℣ *O Gód, my héart is réady, my héart is réa - dy:*

Choir
Lórd,
I will síng, and give práise with the bést mém - ber

Full
héar my voice.   Al - le - lú - ia.
thát I have.

Offertory   Tone II

Cantors
By the wá-ters of Bá-by-lon we sat dówn, and wépt:

Choir
when we re-mém-ber'd thée, O Sý - on.

Communion Tone I

Cantors

Re - mém-ber thy wórd unto thy sérvant, O Lórd,

whérein thou hast cáused me to pút my trúst:

Choir

the sáme is my cómfort in my af - flíc - tion.

713 TRINITY XXI

Introit Tone VII

Cantors

O Lórd Almíghty, éverything is in subjéction

unto thée; and thére is nó man that is áble

Choir

to re - síst thy pów-er: for thóu hast créated

éverything; héaven and éarth, and áll the wónders

which únder héaven's váult are contáined;

FINE

thóu art the Lórd and Kíng of áll things.

Cantors

Ps. Bléss-ed are thóse that are únde-fíl-ed in the wáy:

TRINITY XXI (continued)

Choir

and walk in the law of the Lórd.   *Cantors* Glo-ry   be.....

and tó   the   Hó - ly   Ghóst.   *Choir* As   it

wás.....and év-er shall be: world with-óut énd.

Full A - men.   O   Lórd   Almighty *(etc.)*

Gradual   Tone V

Cantors Lórd, thou hast béen our ré-fuge: *Choir* from óne generátion

to a-nó - ther.   *Cantors* ℣. Be-fóre the móuntains were

bróught fórth, or éver the éarth and the world were máde:

Choir thóu art Gód from éverlásting, and world with-óut énd.

Alleluia   Tone V-I

Cantors Al - le - lu - ia.   *Choir* Al - le - lu - ia.

Cantors ℣. Práise the Lórd, O my sóul, while I líve will I práise the Lórd:
℣. When Ís - rael came óut of   É - gypt:

Choir

yéa, as lóng as I have ány béing, I will síng práises

and the hóuse of Jácob from amóng

Full

ún - to mý Gód. Al - le -lú - ia.

the stránge péo - ple.

Offertory   Tone II

Cántors

There was a mán in the lánd of Úz, whose náme

Choir

was Jób: pér-fect and úpright, and óne that féar-ed God.

Cántors   *Choir*

And Sá-tan sóught to témpt him: and pówer

was gíven him by the Lórd over his posséssions, and

Cántors

ó - ver his flésh. And he de-stróy-ed áll his súb-stance

Choir

and his sóns: and he smóte his flésh with sóre bóils.

Communion   Tone I

Cantors

My sóul hath lónged for thý salvátion;

and I have a góod hópe in thý wórd:

TRINITY XXI (continued)

Choir
whén wilt thóu be avénged of thém that

Cantors
pér-se - cute me? They pér-se - cute me fálse-ly:

Choir
O be thóu my help, O Lórd my Gód.

714   TRINITY XXII

Introit   Tone VII

Cantors
If thóu, O Lórd, wilt be extréme to márk

iníquities, Lórd, whó may a-bíde it: *Choir* for ún - to

thée belóngeth mércy, O Gód of Ís - ra - el. *FINE*

Cantors
Ps. Out of the déep have I cálled ún-to thée, O Lórd:

Choir Lórd, héar my vóice. *Cantors* Gló-ry be.... and to the

Choir Hó-ly Ghóst. As it wás...and év-er sháll be:

Full wórld with-óut énd. A - men. If thóu, O Lórd *(etc.)*

Gradual Tone V

Be-hóld, how góod and jóy-ful a thíng it is:

bré-thren, to dwéll to-gé-ther in ú - ni - ty.

℣. It is líke the précious óint - ment up - ón

the héad: that ran dówn unto the béard,

é - ven ún - to Áa - ron's béard.

Alleluia Tone VI

Al - le - lú - ia. Al - le - lú - ia.

℣. He héal-eth thóse that are bró-ken in héart:
℣. *Ye that féar the Lórd, put your trúst in hím:*

and bínd-eth úp their wóunds.
hé is their hélper and de - fénd - er.

Al - le - lú - ia.

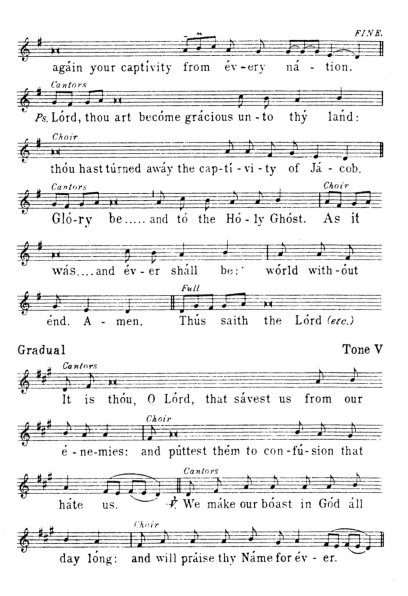

FINE.

agáin your captívity from év-ery ná - tion.

Cantors

Ps. Lórd, thou art becóme grácious un-to thý land:

Choir

thóu hast túrned awáy the cap-tí-vi-ty of Já - cob.

Cantors   *Choir*

Gló-ry be..... and tó the Hó-ly Ghóst. As it

wás....and év-er sháll be:' wórld with-óut

Full

énd. A - men. Thús saith the Lórd *(etc.)*

Gradual   Tone V

Cantors

It is thóu, O Lórd, that sávest us from our

Choir

é - ne-mies: and púttest thém to con-fú-sion that

Cantors

háte us. ℣. We máke our bóast in Gód áll

Choir

day lóng: and will práise thy Náme for év - er.

Alleluia   Tone VI

Cantors   *Choir*

Al - le - lú - ia.   Al - le - lú - ia.

Cantors

He má-keth péace in thy   bór - ders:
Out of the déep have I cálled unto thée, O   Lórd:

Choir

and fílleth thee with the flóur of whéat.
Lórd, héar my vóice.

Full

Al - le - lú - ia.

Offertory   Tone II

Cantors

'Out of the déep have I cáll-ed un - to

Choir

thée, O Lórd: Lórd, héar my vóice.

Communion   Tone I

Cantors

Vé - ri - ly I sáy unto you, whát things

soéver ye de - síre, when ye práy:

Choir

be - líeve that yé recéive them, and it

shall be dóne un - to you.

716   DEDICATION OF A CHURCH

Introit   Tone VII

Cantors

O how dréadful is this pláce! thís is the hóuse

Choir

of Gód, and gáte of héa‑ven: and mén shall cáll it

FINE Cantors

the pá‑lace of Gód. **Ps.** The Lórd is Kíng, and
               Ps. *O how ámiable are*

Choir

hath pút on gló‑rious ap‑pá‑rel: the Lórd hath
thy   *dwéll‑ings, thou Lórd of hósts: my sóul hath a*

pút on his appárel, and gird‑ed him‑sélf with
desire and lónging to énter into the cóurts of the

Cantors

stréngth. Gló‑ry be . . . and to the Ho‑ly Ghóst.
Lórd.

Choir

As it wás . . . and év‑er sháll be: wórld with‑óut

Full

énd. A‑men. O how dréadful *(etc.)*

Gradual   Tone V

Cantors   *Choir*

This dwéll‑ing is Gód's hán‑dy‑wórk: it is a mýstery

beyónd all príce, that cán‑not be spó‑ken a‑gáinst.

DEDICATION OF A CHURCH (continued)

Cantors

℣. O Gód, in whose présence the chóirs of Án-gels are stánd-ing:

Choir

grá-cious-ly héar the práyers of thy sér - vants.

Alleluia　　　　　　　　　　　　　　　　**Tone VI**

Cantors　　　　*Choir*

Al - le - lú - ia.　Al - le - lú - ia.

Cantors　　　　　　　　　　*Choir*

℣. I will wórship towárd thy hóly tém-ple:　and will síng práises

Full

un-to thy Náme. Al - le - lú - ia.

Between Septuagesima and Easter, instead of Alleluia, *is sung the following:*

Tract　　　　　　　　　　　　　　　　**Tone VIII**

Cantors

Théy that trúst in the Lórd shall be éven as the móunt Sý-on:

which máy not bé remóved, but stándeth fást for　év - er.

Choir

℣. The hílls stánd abóut Je-rú-sa-lem:　éven só stándeth the Lórd

róund abóut his péople, from thís time fórth for　év - er-more.

During Easter-tide the Gradual is omitted. The foregoing Alleluia *is sung, followed at once by:*

Cantors　　　　　　　　　　　　　*Choir*

℣. The hóuse of God is súrely fóund-ed:　stá - blish-ed

Full

up - ón the róck. Al - le -lú - ia.

Offertory Tone II

Cantors

O Lórd Gód, in the úpríghtness of my héart I have wíllingly

Choir

óf - fer - ed áll these thíngs:and nów I have séen with jóy thy péople,

Cantors

which are pré-sent hére.   O Lórd Gód of Ísrael, kéep for éver

Choir

this i - má - gi - ná - tion: of the héart of thy péo-ple.

Communion Tone I

Cantors

My hóuse shall be cálled of áll nátions the hóuse of práyer, sáith

Choir

the Lórd: in it évery one that ásketh recéiveth, and hé that séek-

Cantors   *Choir*

-eth fínd-eth. And to him that knóck-eth: it shall be ó-pen-ed.

717 ON THE FEAST OF AN APOSTLE OR EVANGELIST
Introit OUT OF EASTER-TIDE   Tone VII

Cantors

(i) Right déar, O Gód, are thy fríends unto me, and héld in
(ii) *The móuth of the ríghteous is éxer -*

Choir

high-est hó - nour: their rúle and góvernance is
- cis - ed in wis - dom: and his tóngue will he tálking

FINE

ex - céed-ing stéad - fast.
of júdgement; the láw of his Gód   is   ín his   héart.

Introit (i) is generally used on all feasts of Apostles and Evangelists out of Easter -
tide, except on the Feast of St. Matthew when (ii) is used according to the Western
Rite.

ON THE FEAST OF AN APOSTLE etc. (continued)

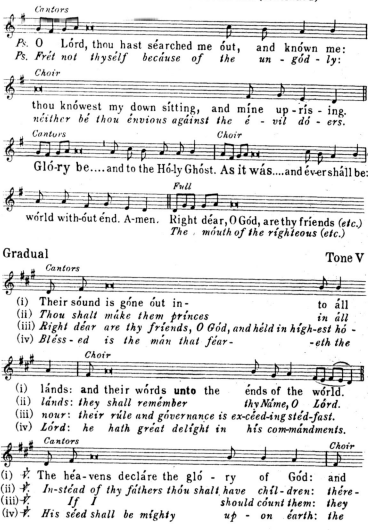

Cantors

Ps. O Lórd, thou hast séarched me óut,   and knówn me:
Ps. Frét not thysélf becáuse of the   un - gód - ly:

Choir

thou knówest my down sítting,   and míne up-rís - ing.
néither bé thou énvious agáinst the é - vil dó - ers.

Cantors   *Choir*

Gló-ry be.... and to the Hó-ly Ghóst. As it wás....and éver shâll be:

Full

wórld with-óut énd. A-men.   Right déar, O Gód, are thy friends *(etc.)*
          The   móuth of the ríghteous *(etc.)*

Gradual

Tone V

Cantors

(i) Their sóund is góne óut in-   to áll
(ii) Thou shalt máke them prínces   in áll
(iii) Right déar are thy friends, O Gód, and héld in híghest hó -
(iv) Bléss-ed is the mán that féar-   -eth the

Choir

(i) lánds: and their wórds **unto** the   énds of the wórld.
(ii) lánds: they shall remémber   thy Náme, O Lórd.
(iii) nour: their rúle and góvernance is ex-céed-ing stéd-fast.
(iv) Lórd: he hath gréat delíght in his com-mándments.

Cantors   *Choir*

(i) ℣. The héa-vens declére the gló - ry   of Gód: and
(ii) ℣. In-stéad of thy fáthers thóu shalt have chíl-dren: thére-
(iii) ℣.   If I   should cóunt them: they
(iv) ℣. His séed shall be míghty   up - on éarth: the

Gradual (i) is given in the *English Hymnal* for general use. According to the Western
Rite it is used only on the feasts of St. Barnabas & St. Luke. According to the same
Rite (ii) is used on the feasts of St. Andrew, St. James, St. Bartholomew and SS. Simon
& Jude, (iii) on the feasts of St. Thomas & St. Matthias, and (iv) the feast of St. Matthew.

(i) the firmament shew-eth his han-di-work.
(ii) *fore shall the people give thanks un-to thee.*
(iii) *are more in number than the sand of the sea.*
(iv) *generation of the faithful shall be bless - ed.*

Alleluia   Tone VI

Cantors   *Choir*

Al - le - lú - ia. Al - le - lú - ia.

Cantors

(i) ℣. I first will say to Syon, Behold, be- hold them:
(ii) ℣. *The Lord loved*   An - drew:
(iii) ℣. *Re - joice in the Lord, O ye*   righ-teous:
(iv) ℣. *I have chosen you out of*   the world:
(v) ℣. *The glo - rious company of the A -* pos-tles:
(vi) ℣. *Right dear are they friends unto me, O God, and held in highest ho - nour:*

Choir

(i) and I will give to Jerusalem one that bring-eth good tí - dings.
(ii) *as a sweet-*   smel - ling sa - vour.
(iii) *for it becometh well the just*   to be thank - ful.
(iv) *that ye should go and bring fruit, and that your fruit should re-main.*
(v)   praise thee, O God.
(vi) *their rule and governance is ex - ceed-ing sted - fast.*

Full

Al - le - lú - ia.

Alleluia-verse (i) is given in the *English Hymnal* for general use. According to the Western Rite (ii) is used on the feast of St. Andrew, (iii) on the feast of St. Thomas, (iv) on the feasts of St. Barnabas, St. James, & St. Luke, (v) on the feasts of St. Bartholomew & St. Matthew, and (vi) on the feast of SS. Simon & Jude.

Tract　　ON THE FEAST OF AN APOSTLE etc. (continued)　　Tone VIII

Cantors

(i) Bléss-ed is the mán that féareth the Lórd: hé hath gréat delíght in
(ii) *Thóu hast gíven him his héart's de - síre: and hast nót deníed him*

Choir

his com - mánd-ments. ℣ His séed shall be míghty upon
the requést of hís líps. ℣. For thóu shalt prevént him with the bléss-

éarth:　　the géneration of the fáithful shall be bléss - ed.
-ings of góod-ness: and shalt sét a crówn of púre góld up - ón his héad.

Offertory　　　　　　　　　　　　　　　　　　　Tone II

Cantors

(i) Thóu shalt máke them
(ii) *Right déar are thy friends unto mé, O Gód, and héld*
(iii) *Their sóund is góne*
(iv) *Thóu hast sét, O Lórd, a crówn of*

Choir

(i) prín-ces in áll lánds: théy shall remémber thy Náme,
(ii) *in high-est hó - nour: their rúle and góvernance is*
(iii) *óut in - to áll lánds: and their wórds únto*
(iv) *púre góld up-ón his héad: he ásk - ed lífe of thée, and*

(i) O Lórd, from óne generá - tion to a - nó - ther.
(ii) *ex - céed-ing stéd - fast.*
(iii) *the énds of the wórld.*
(iv) *thou gávest him a lóng lífe, al - le - lú - ia.*

Communion   Tone I

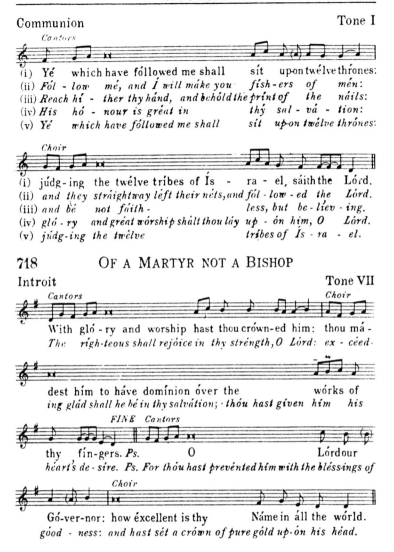

(i) Ye̒ which have fóllowed me shall sít upon twélve thrónes:
(ii) Fól - low me̒, and I will máke you físh-ers of mén:
(iii) Reach hí - ther thy hánd, and behóld the prínt of the náils:
(iv) His hó - nour is gréat in thy̒ sal - vá - tion:
(v) Ye̒ which have fóllowed me shall sít up-on twélve thrónes:

(i) júdg-ing the twélve tríbes of Ís - ra - el, sáith the Lórd.
(ii) and they stráightway léft their néts, and fól - low - ed the Lórd.
(iii) and bé not fáith- less, but be - líev - ing.
(iv) gló - ry and gréat wórship shált thou láy up - ón him, O Lórd.
(v) júdg-ing the twélve tríbes of Ís - ra - el.

718   OF A MARTYR NOT A BISHOP

Introit   Tone VII

With gló - ry and worship hast thou crówn-ed him: thou má -
The̒ rígh-teous shall rejóice in thy stréngth, O Lórd: ex - céed-

dest hím to háve domínion óver the wórks of
ing glád shall he bé in thy salvátion; · thóu hast gíven him his

FINE

thy fín-gers. Ps.   O   Lórd our
héart's de - síre. Ps. For thóu hast prevénted hím with the bléss-ings of

Gó-ver-nor: how éxcellent is thy Náme in áll the wórld.
góod - ness: and hast sét a crówn of púre góld up-ón his héad.

Communion (i) is given in the *English Hymnal* for general use. According to the Western Rite (i) is used on the feast of St. Bartholomew, (ii) on the feast of St. Andrew, (iii)
on the feast of St. Thomas, (iv) on the feast of St. Matthew, and (v) on the feasts of
St. Matthias, St. Barnabas, St. James, St. Luke, and SS. Simon and Jude.

OF A MARTYR NOT A BISHOP (continued)

Cantors   *Choir*

Gló-ry be... and to the Hó-ly Ghóst. As it wás....and év-er

Full

sháll be: wórld with-óut énd. A-men. With gló - ry *(etc.)*
     The rígh-teous *(etc.)*

Gradual   **Tone V**

Cantors   *Choir*

Thóu hast sét, O Lórd: a crówn of pure
Bléss-ed is the mán that féar-eth the Lórd: hé hath gréat delíght

Cantors

góld up-ón his héad. ℣. Thou hast gív-en him his héart's
in hís com-mánd-ments. ℣. His séed shall be mígh-ty up-ón

Choir

de-síre: and hast nót denied him the re-quést of his líps.
éarth: the géneration of the fáithful shall be bléss-ed.

Alleluia   **Tone VI**

Cantors   *Choir*   *Cantors*

Al - le-lú-ia. Al - le-lú-ia.   ℣. Thóu hast sét a

Choir   *Full*

crówn of púre góld: up-ón his héad, O Lórd. Al - le-lú-ia.

Between Septuagesima and Easter, instead of Alleluia, is sung the following.

Tract   **Tone VIII**

Cantors

Thóu hast gíven him his héart's de-síre: and hast nót deníed him

Choir

the requést of his líps. ℣. For thóu hast prevénted him with the bléss-

ings of góod-ness: and hast sét a crówn of pure góld up-ón his héad.

Offertory   Tone II

With glo-ry and wor-ship hast thou crown-ed him: thou ma-dest him

to have dominion over the works of thy fin-gers, O   Lord.

Communion   Tone I

He that   will come after me, let him   de - ny   him - self:

and   take   up   his   cross,   and   fol - low   me.

719   OF AN APOSTLE OR MARTYR
                            IN EASTER-TIDE
Introit   (including ST. GEORGE and ST. MARK)   Tone VII

Thou hast hidden me, O God, from the gathering together of the

froward, al-le-lu - ia: from the insurrection of the workers

of iniquity, al-le-lu-ia,   al-le-lu - ia. *Ps.* Hear my

voice, O God, in my prayer: preserve my life from fear of the e-ne-my.

Glo-ry be.... and to the Ho-ly Ghost. As it   was....and ev-er

shall be: world with-out end A-men. Thou hast hidden me (*etc.*)

OF AN APOSTLE OR MARTYR etc. (continued)

Alleluia   **Tone VI**

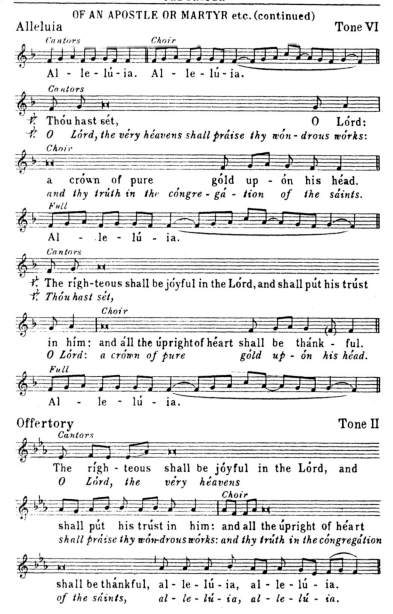

Cantors   *Choir*

Al - le - lú - ia.   Al - le - lú - ia.

Cantors

℣. Thóu hast sét,   O   Lórd:
℣. *O Lórd, the véry héavens shall práise thy wón - drous wórks:*

Choir

a   crówn   of   pure   góld   up - ón   his   héad.
and thy trúth in the cóngre - gá - tion   of   the   sáints.

Full

Al   -   le - lú - ia.

Cantors

℣. The righ-teous shall be jóyful in the Lórd, and shall pút his trúst
℣. *Thóu hast sét,*

Choir

in him: and áll the úpright of héart shall be   thánk - ful.
O Lórd: a crówn of pure   góld up - ón   his héad.

Full

Al   -   le - lú - ia.

Offertory   **Tone II**

Cantors

The   rígh - teous   shall be jóyful   in the Lórd,   and
O   Lórd, the   véry   héavens

Choir

shall pút   his trúst in   him: and all the úpright of héart
shall práise thy wón-drous wórks: and thy trúth in the cóngregátion

shall be thánkful, al - le - lú - ia, al - le - lú - ia.
of the sáints,   al - le - lú - ia,   al - le - lú - ia.

Communion   Tone I

Hé that will come áfter me, lét   him de - ný
The righ - teous shall rejóice in the Lórd, and pút his trúst

him - sélf: and táke up his cróss, and fóllow me,
in   hím: and áll théy that are trúe of héart shall be gláḍ,

al - le - lú - ia,   al - le - lú - ia.
al - le - lú - ia,   al - le - lú - ia.

720   OF A BISHOP AND CONFESSOR
Introit   (including ST. DAVID and ST. PATRICK)   Tone VII

The   Lórd hath estáblished a cóvenant of péace with him,

and máde him a chíef of his péo-ple: that hé should háve

FINE

the priestly dígnity for   év - er and év - er.

Ps. My   sóng shall be ál - way: of the lóving-kínd-ness
Ps. Lórd, re - mém-ber Dá - vid: and   áll   his

of the Lórd. Gló - ry..... and to the Hó - ly Ghóst.
tróu - ble.

As it wás...and év-er sháll be: wórld with-óut énd A - men.

The   Lórd   hath   estáblished *(etc.)*

OF A BISHOP AND CONFESSOR (continued)

Gradual   Tone V

Cantors   *Choir*

Be-hóld, a mígh-ty pré - late: who in his lífetime was pléas-ing ún - to Gód.   ℣. There was nóne found líke ún-to him: that obsérved the láw of the Móst High.

Alleluia   Tone VI

Cantors   *Choir*

Al - le - lú - ia.   Al - le - lú - ia.

Cantors   *Choir*

℣. The rígh-teous shall blóssom as the lí -ly : and shall flóurish for

℣. *Thóu art a príest for*   *év-er : áfter the órder*

Full

év-er befóre the Lórd. Al - le - lú - ia.

of Mel-chi-se - dech.

Between Septuagesima and Easter, instead of **Alleluia**, *is sung the following.*

Tract   Tone VIII

Cantors

Bléss-ed is the mán that féareth the Lórd: hé hath gréat delíght in

Choir

his com-mand-ments. ℣. His séed shall be míghty upon éarth: the

Cantors

géneration of the fáithful shall be bléss-ed. ℣. Ríches and plénte-

Choir

ousness shall bé in his hóuse: and his ríghteousness endúreth for év-er.

During Easter-tide the foregoing Gradual *and* Alleluia *are omitted, and the following is sung:*

Alleluia
Tone VI

Cantors   *Choir*

Al - le - lú - ia. Al - le - lú - ia.

Cantors   *Choir*

℣. Thóu art a príest for év - er: áfter the órder

Full

of Mel-chí-se-dech. Al - le - lú - ia.

Cantors   *Choir*

℣. This is a príest: whom the Lórd hath crówn - ed.

Full

Al - le - lú - ia.

Offertory
Tone II

Cantors

My trúth ál - so and my   mer -

I have fóund Dávid my sérvant, with my hóly óil

Choir

cy sháll be wíth him: and ín my Náme

have I a-nóint-ed him: my hánd shall hóld

shall his hórn be ex - ált - ed.

him fást, and my árm shall stréng - then him.

Communion
Tone I

Cantors

Hé that wíll come áfter me, lét   him de-ný

A fáith-ful and wíse stéward, whom the Lórd made rúler ó-ver his

Choir

him-sélf: and táke up his cróss, and fól-low me.

house-hold: to gíve them their pórtion of méat in dúe séa-son.

721   OF A MARTYR BISHOP

Introit   Tono VII

O ye priests of the Lord, bless ye the Lord: O ye

FINE

holy and humble men of heart, ex-alt him for ev - er.

Ps. O all ye works of the Lord, bless ye the Lord: praise him,

and magnify him for ev - er. Glo - ry be.....

and to the Ho-ly Ghost. As is was... and ev-er shall be:

world with-out end, A - men. O ye priests of the Lord *(etc.)*

Gradual   Tone V

Thou hast crowned him with glo-ry and wor-ship: thou hast made

him to have dominion of the works of thy hands, O Lord.

Alleluia   Tone VI

Al - le - lú - ia. Al - le - lú - ia.

℣. The Lord loved him, and adorn-ed him: and clothed him with a

℣. *This is*   *the priest: whom the*

robe of glo - ry. Al - le - lú - ia.
Lord hath cho - sen.

Betueen Septuagesima and Easter, instead of Alleluia, *is sung the Tract* Blessed is the man *(page 166)*

Offertory – I have found David *(page 167)*

Communion
Tone I

Cantors *Choir*

Thou hast set a crown of pure gold: up-on his head, O Lord.

722 OF A CONFESSOR NOT A BISHOP

Introit Tone VII

Cantors

The mouth of the righteous is exercised in wisdom, and his

Choir

tongue will be talk-ing of e-qui-ty: the law of his God

FINE Cantors

is in his heart. Ps. Fret not thy-self be-cause of the un-god-ly:

Choir *Cantors*

neither be thou envious against the e-vil do-ers. Glo-ry be....

Choir

and to the Ho-ly Ghost. As it was.... and ev-er shall be:

Full

world with-out end. A - men. The mouth of the righteous *(etc.)*

Gradual Tone V

Cantors

I have found David my servant, with my holy oil have
The righ-teous shall flourish

Choir

I a-noint-ed him: my hand shall hold him fast, and my
like a palm - tree: and shall spread abroad like a cedar in

arm shall streng-then him.
Libanus in the house of the Lord.

OF A CONFESSOR NOT A BISHOP (continued)

℣. The e - nemy shall nót be able to dó him ví - o - lence:
℣. To téll of thy lóving-kíndness éarly in the mórn - ing:

the són of wickedness sháll not húrt him.
and of thy trúth in the níght-séa - son.

Alleluia   Tone VI

Al - le - lú - ia. Al - le - lú - ia.

℣. I have laíd hélp upon óne that is mígh - ty:
℣. Bléss-ed is the mán that endúreth temp - tá - tion:

I have exálted one chósen óut of the péo - ple.
for whén he is tríed hé shall re-céive a crówn of life.

Al - le - lú - ia.

Between Septuagesima and Easter, instead of **Alleluia,** *is sung the Tract* **Blessed is the man** *(page 166)*
During Easter-tide the Gradual is omitted, The foregoing **Alleluia** *is sung, followed at once by:*

The Lórd lóved him and a-dórn-ed him: he clóthed him with a

róbe of gló - ry. Al - le - lú - ia.

Offertory- My truth also and my mercy *(see page 167)*

Communion   Tone I

Cantors

Lórd, thou delíveredst únto   me fíve tá - lents:
Bléss - ed   is that sérvant whóm his Lórd shall fínd wátch-ing:

Choir

be - hóld, I have gáined besíde   them
vé - ri - ly I say unto yóu, that hé shall máke him rúler ó -

Cantors

fíve tá - lents more. Wéll dóne, góod and faíthful sérvant, thóu
-ver áll his góods.

Choir

hast been faíthful ó - ver a féw thíngs: Í will máke thee rúler

óver mány thíngs, énter thóu into the   jóy of thy   Lórd.

723   OF A VIRGIN MARTYR

Introit   Tone VII

Cantors

I   have spóken of thy téstimonies in the síght of

Choir

prínces, and was nót con-fóund-ed: and my delíght hath

FINE

béen in thy commándments, which Í have lúv-ed gréat-ly.

Cantors

Ps. Bléss - ed   are thóse that are únde-fí - led in the wáy:

Choir

and wálk in the láw of the Lórd.

OF A VIRGIN MARTYR (continued)

Cantors
Gló - ry be..... and to the Hó - ly Ghóst.

Choir
As it wás.....and év-er sháll be: wórld with -

Full
óut énd. A - men. I have spóken *(etc.)*

Gradual   Tone V

Cantors   *Choir*
Thóu hast lóv - ed rígh-teous-ness: and há - ted

Cantors
i - ní - qui - ty.   ℣. Whére-fore Gód, é-ven thý Gód:

Choir
hath anoínted thée with the óil of glád - ness.

Alleluia   Tone VI

Cantors   *Choir*
Al - le - lú - ia. Al - le - lú - ia.

Cantors
℣. Fúll of gráce are   thy líps:
℣. *The vir - gins that bé her féllows shall be bróught un-to thée:*

Choir
becáuse Gód hath bléssed thée for év - er.
with jóy and glád - ness shall théy be bróught.

Full
Al - le - lú - ia.

Between Septuagesima and Easter, instead of Alleluia, *is sung the following:*

Tract · Tone VIII

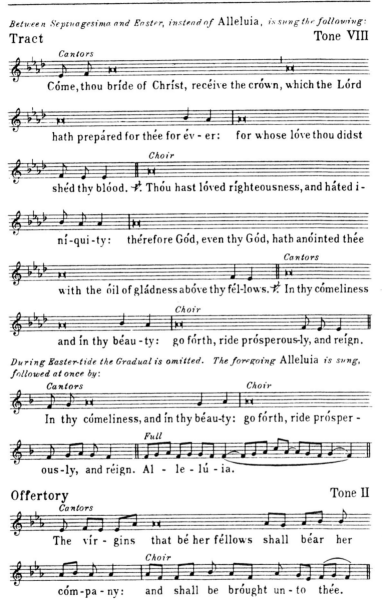

Cantors

Cóme, thou bríde of Christ, recéive the crówn, which the Lórd

hath prepáred for thée for év - er: for whose lóve thou didst

Choir

shéd thy blóod. ℣. Thóu hast lóved ríghteousness, and háted i-

ní-qui-ty: thérefore Gód, even thy Gód, hath anóinted thée

Cantors

with the óil of gládness abóve thy fél-lows. ℣. In thy cómeliness

Choir

and ín thy béau - ty: go fórth, ride prósperous-ly, and reígn.

During Easter-tide the Gradual is omitted. The foregoing Alleluia *is sung, followed at once by:*

Cantors · *Choir*

In thy cómeliness, and ín thy béau-ty: go fórth, ride prósper -

Full

ous-ly, and reígn. Al - le - lú - ia.

Offertory · Tone II

Cantors

The vír - gins that bé her féllows shall béar her

Choir

cóm-pa - ny: and shall be bróught un - to thée.

OF A VIRGIN MARTYR (continued)

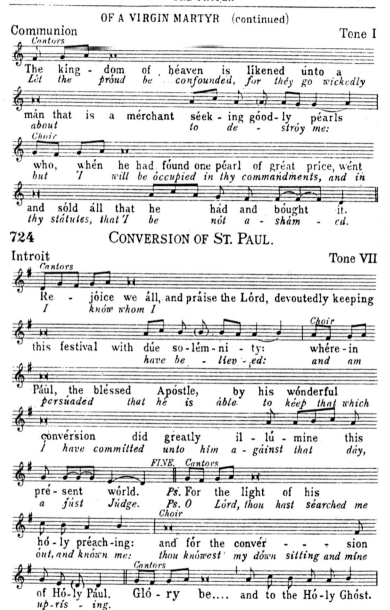

Communion　　　　　　　　　　　　　　　Tone I

Cantors

The king - dom of heaven is likened unto a
Let the proud be confounded, for they go wickedly

man that is a merchant seek - ing good- ly pearls
about　　　　　　to　de　-　stroy me:

Choir

who, when he had found one pearl of great price, went
but　'I　will be occupied in thy commandments, and in

and sold all that he had and bought　it.
thy statutes, that 'I be　not a - sham - ed.

724　　　CONVERSION OF ST. PAUL.

Introit　　　　　　　　　　　　　　　Tone VII

Cantors

Re - joice we all, and praise the Lord, devoutedly keeping
I　know whom I

this festival with due so - lem - ni - ty:　where - in
have be - liev - ed:　and am

Choir

Paul, the blessed Apostle, by his wonderful
persuaded　that he is　able　to keep that which

conversion did greatly il - lu - mine this
I have committed unto him a - gainst that day,

FIVE. Cantors

pre - sent world. *Ps.* For the light of his
a just Judge. *Ps.* O Lord, thou hast searched me

Choir

ho - ly preach -ing: and for the conver - - - sion
out, and known me: thou knowest my down sitting and mine

Cantors

of Ho-ly Paul. Glo - ry be.... and to the Ho-ly Ghost.
up-ris - ing.

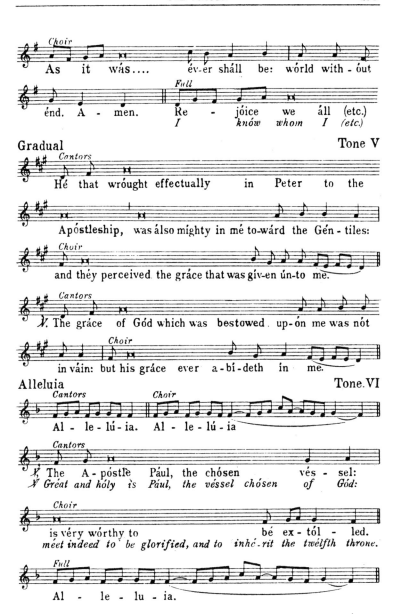

As it was.... év-er shall be: world with - out end. A - men.

Re - jóice we all (etc.)
I knów whom I (etc.)

Gradual   Tone V

Hé that wróught effectually in Peter to the Apóstleship, was álso míghty in mé to-wárd the Gén - tiles: and théy perceived the gráce that was gív-en ún-to mé.

℣. The gráce of Gód which was bestowed. up-ón me was nót in váin: but his gráce ever a - bí - deth ín mé.

Alleluia   Tone. VI

Al - le - lú - ia. Al - le - lú - ia.

℣. The A - póstle Pául, the chósen vés - sel:
℣ Gréat and hóly is Pául, the véssel chósen of Gód:

is véry wórthy to bé ex - tól - led.
méet indeed to be glorified, and to inhé - rit the twélfth throne.

Al - le - lu - ia.

CONVERSION OF St. PAUL (continued)

Offertory   Tono II

Cantors

O how déar are thy friends un - to mé. O Gód:

Choir

O how gréat is the pre-ém-in - ence of thém.

Communion   Tone I

Cantors

A-men, I sáy unto yóu, that yé which háve forsaken

Choir

áll, and fól-low-ed mé: shall re - céive an hundredfold,

and sháll in - hé - rit év - er-lást - ing. life.

725   THE PURIFICATION

Introit as at N⁰ 700 (page 115)

Gradual   Tone V

Cantors

We have wáited, O Gód, for thy lóving - kindness

Choir

in the midst of thy tém - ple: ac - córding to thy Náme,

O Gód, só is thy práise un-to the wórld's énd.

Cantors

℣ Like as wé have héard, só have we séen in the city

Choir

of our Gód: é-ven up-ón his hó-ly hill.

Alleluia   Tone VI

Al - le - lú - ia   Al - le - lú - ia.,

℣ I will worship towárd thy hóly tém - ple,   and will sing práises
℟ The óld mán cárried   the   Child: but the Child góvern-

ún-to   thý Náme.   Al - le - lú - ia.
.ed the   óld mán.

If the Feast falls after Septuagesima, instead of the Alleluia the following is sung:

Tract   Tone VIII

Lórd, now léttest thóu thy sérvant depárt   in   péace:

accórding to thý wórd. ℣ For mine éyes have   séen: thy sal-

vá-tion ℣ Which thóu hast pre-pár - ed: befóre the fáce of áll

péo - ple. ℣ To be a light to líghten the Gén - tiles.

and to be the glory of thy people 'Is - ra - el.

Offertory   Tone II

Fúll of   gráce   are   thy   lips: be - cáuse

Gód hath bléss - ed thée for év - er.

THE PURIFICATION (continued)

Communion   Tone I

Cantors

It was revéaled unto Simeon by the Hó - ly

Choir

Spi - ri̇t: that hé should nót see déath, before

he had séen the Lórds A - nóint - ed.

725   THE ANNUNCIATION

Introit   Tone VII

Cantors

Drop   dówn, ye heáv- ens, from abóve, and lét the skies
The   rich also amóng the péople shall máke their súpplicátion

befóre thee, shé shall be bróught únto the Kíng in a

póur down rígh - teous-ness: lét the éarth ópen, and
rái-ment of née - dle - work: the vír-gins that bé her

Choir

let her   bring fórth sal-
féllows shall be bróught unto thée; with jóy and

FINE. Cantors

va - tion. *Ps.* And let righteousness·spring úp to-gé -ther:
glád - ness. Ps. My héart is inditing of a góod mát-ter:

Choir

'I the Lórd   have cre-á-ted it.
I spéak of the thíngs which I have máde un-tó the Kíng.

Cantors

Gló - ry be.... and to the Hó- ly Ghóst.

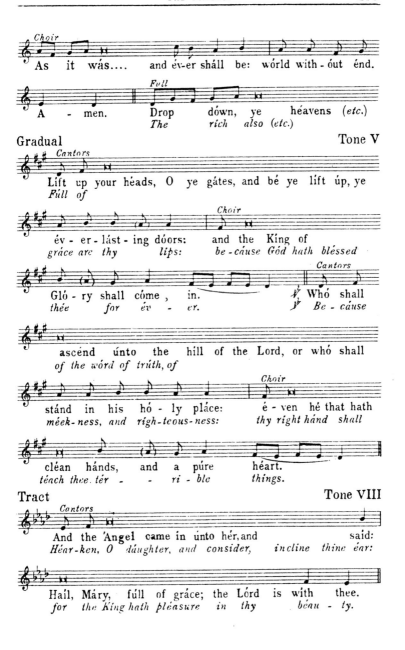

Choir

As it wás.... and ev-er sháll be: wórld with-óut énd.

A - men. **Full** Drop dówn, ye héavens *(etc.)*
The rich also (etc.)

Gradual Tone V

Cantors

Líft up your héads, O ye gátes, and bé ye líft úp, ye
Fúll of

Choir

év - er-lást-ing dóors: and the Kíng of
gráce are thy lips: be-cáuse Gód hath bléssed

Cantors

Gló - ry shall cóme , in. ℣ Whó shall
thée for év - er. ℟ Be - cáuse

ascénd únto the hill of the Lord, or whó shall
of the wórd of trúth, of

Choir

stánd in his hó - ly pláce: é - ven hé that hath
méek-ness, and rígh-teous-ness: thy right hánd shall

cléan hánds, and a púre héart.
téach thee. tér - - ri - ble things.

Tract Tone VIII

Cantors

And the 'Angel came in únto hér, and said:
Héar-ken, O dáughter, and consider, incline thine éar:

Haíl, Máry, fúll of gráce; the Lórd is with thee.
for the Kíng hath pléasure in thy béau - ty.

THE ANNUNCIATION (continued)

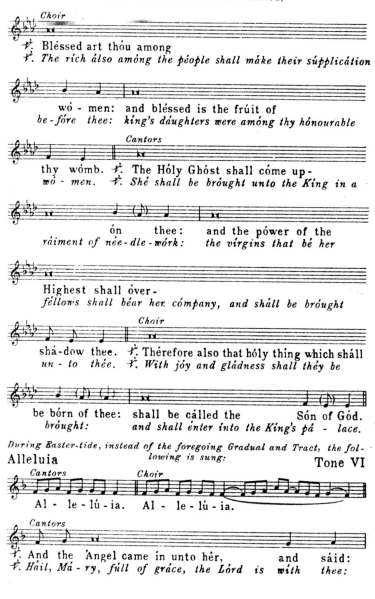

℣. Bléssed art thóu among
℣. *The rích álso amóng the péople shall máke their súpplicátion*

wó - men: and bléssed is the frúit of
be - fóre thee: kíng's dáughters were amóng thy hónourable

thy wómb. ℣. The Hóly Ghóst shall cóme up-
wó - men. ℣. Shé shall be bróught unto the Kíng in a

ón thee: and the pówer of the
ráiment of née-dle-wórk: the vírgins that bé her

Highest shall óver-
féllows shall béar her cómpany, and sháll be bróught

shá-dow thee. ℣. Thérefore also that hóly thíng which sháll
un - to thée. ℣. With jóy and gládness shall théy be

be bórn of thee: shall be cálled the Són of Gód.
bróught: and shall énter ínto the Kíng's pá - lace.

*During Easter-tide, instead of the foregoing Gradual and Tract, the fol-
lowing is sung:*

Alleluia   Tone VI

Al - le - lú - ia. Al - le - lú - ia.

℣. And the 'Angel came ín unto hér, and sáid:
℣. Háil, Má - ry, fúll of gráce, the Lórd is with thee:

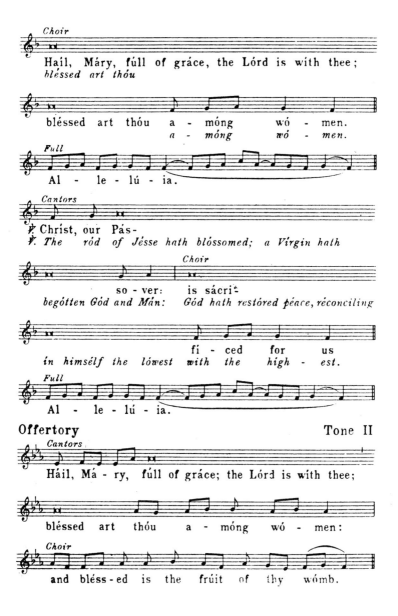

Choir

Hail, Máry, fúll of gráce, the Lórd is with thee;
bléssed art thóu

bléssed art thóu   a - móng   wó - men.
a - móng   wó - men.

Full

Al - le - lú - ia.

Cantors

℣ Christ, our Pás-
℣. The   ród   of Jésse hath blóssomed; a Vírgin hath

Choir

so - ver: is sácri-
begótten Gód and Mán: Gód hath restóred péace, réconciling

fí - ced   for   us
in himsélf the lówest with the   high - est.

Full

Al - le - lú - ia.

Offertory   Tone II

Cantors

Háil, Má - ry,   fúll of gráce; the Lórd is with thee;

bléssed art thóu   a - móng   wó - men:

Choir

and bléss-ed is the   frúit of thy   wómb.

THE ANNUNCIATION (continued)

Communion   Tone I

Be - hóld, a Vírgin shall con - céive, and béar a Són:

and his Náme shall be cáll - ed Em - má - nu - el.

726   ST. PHILIP & ST. JAMES

Introit   Tone VII

They crí - ed unto thée, O Lórd, ín the

tíme of their mí - se - ry and tróu - ble:

and thóu didst héar them from thy hóly héaven,

al - le - lú - ia, al - le - lú - ia.

Ps. Re - jóice in the Lórd, O, ye rígh - teous:

for it becómeth wéll the júst to be thánk - ful.

Gló - ry be . . . and to the Hó - ly Ghóst.

As it wás . . . and év - er sháll be: wórld with -

- óut énd. A - men. They crí - ed unto thée *(etc.)*

Alleluia
Tone VI

Al - le - lú - ia. Al - le - lú - ia.

℣. The righ-teous mán shall stánd in great bóld-ness:
℣. *O Lórd, the véry héavens shall práise thy wón-drous wórks:*

befóre the fáce of súch as háve af - flict - ed him.
and thy trúth in the cóngre - gá - tion of the sáints.

Al - le - lú - ia.

℣. Did not our héart búrn with-
℣. *Háve I béen so lóng time with you, and yét hast*

in us: while he
thóu not knówn me, Phi - lip: hé that

tálked wíth us bý the wáy con-cérn-ing Jé - sus.
hath séen me hath séen my Fá - ther.

Al - le - lú - ia.

Offertory
Tone II

O Lórd, the vé - ry héa -vens shall práise thy

wón - drous wórks: and thy trúth in the cóngregátion

of the sáints, al - le - lú - ia, al - le - lú - ia.

ST. PHILIP & ST. JAMES (continued)

Communion   Tone I

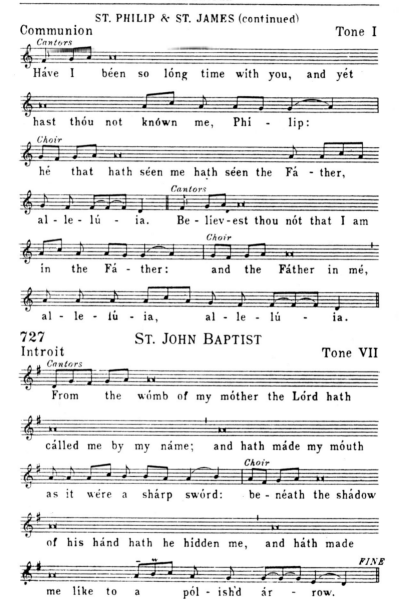

Háve I béen so lóng time with you, and yét

hast thóu not knówn me, Phí - lip:

hé that hath séen me hath séen the Fá - ther,

al - le - lú - ia. Be - liev-est thou nót that I am

in the Fá - ther: and the Fáther in mé,

al - le - lú - ia, al - le - lú - ia.

727 St. John Baptist

Introit   Tone VII

From the wómb of my móther the Lórd hath

cálled me by my náme; and hath máde my móuth

as it wére a shárp swórd: be - néath the shádow

of his hánd hath he hidden me, and háth made

FINE

me like to a pól - ish'd ár - row.

Cantors

Ps. It is a góod thing to give thánks ún-to

Choir

the Lórd: and to sing práises unto thy Náme, O

Cantors

Most High-est. Gló-ry be... and to the Hó-ly Ghóst.

Choir

As it wás... and év-er sháll be: wórld with-

Full

-óut énd. A-men. From the wómb (etc.)

Gradual   **Tone V**

Cantors

Be-fóre I fórmed thee in the bél-ly I

Choir

knéw thee: and befóre thou cámest fórth óut of

the wómb I sánc-ti-fi-ed thee.

Cantors

℟. The Lórd put fórth his hánd and tóuch-ed

Choir

my móuth: and sáid un-to me.

Alleluia   **Tone VI**

Cantors   Choir

Al-le-lú-ia. Al-le-lú-ia.

ST. JOHN BAPTIST (continued)

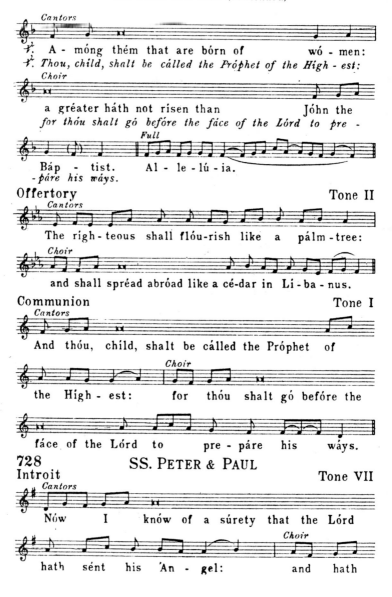

Cantors

℣. A - móng thém that are bórn of wó - men:
℣. *Thou, child, shalt be cálled the Próphet of the High - est:*

Choir

a gréater háth not rísen than Jóhn the
for thóu shalt gó befóre the fáce of the Lórd to pre -

Full

Báp - tist. Al - le - lú - ia.
- páre his wáys.

Offertory   Tone II

Cantors

The righ - teous shall flóu-rish like a pálm - tree:

Choir

and shall spréad abróad like a cé-dar in Lí - ba - nus.

Communion   Tone I

Cantors

And thóu, child, shalt be cálled the Próphet of

Choir

the Hígh - est: for thóu shalt gó befóre the

fáce of the Lórd to pre - páre his wáys.

728   SS. PETER & PAUL
Introit   Tone VII

Cantors

Nów I knów of a súrety that the Lórd

Choir

hath sént his 'An - gel: and hath

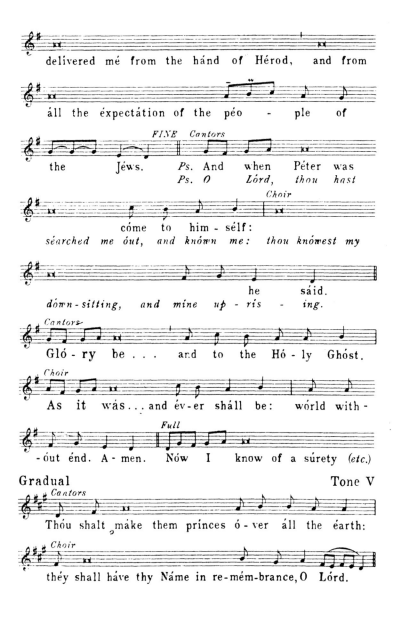

delivered mé from the hánd of Hérod, and from

áll the expectátion of the péo - ple of

the Jéws. *FINE* *Cantors*
Ps. And when Péter was
Ps. O Lórd, thou hast

Choir
cóme to him - sélf:
séarched me óut, and knówn me: thou knówest my

he sáid.
dówn - sitting, and mine up - rís - ing.

Cantors
Gló - ry be . . . and to the Hó - ly Ghóst.

Choir
As it wás... and év - er shall be: world with -

Full
- óut énd. A - men. Nów I know of a súrety (*etc.*)

Gradual Tone V

Cantors
Thóu shalt make them prínces ó - ver áll the éarth:

Choir
théy shall háve thy Náme in re - mém - brance, O Lórd.

SS. PETER & PAUL (continued)

Cantors
℣. In - stéad of thy fáthers thóu shalt

Choir
have chíl - dren: thére - fore shall the

péople give thánks un - to thée.

Alleluia   Tone VI

Cantors   *Choir*
Al - le - lú - ia.   Al - le - lú - ia.

Cantors
℣. Thóu art Símon Bar - Jóna, and to thée hath béen
℣. *Thóu art Péter, and upón*

Choir
revéaled the wórd of the Fá - ther: nót by flésh and
this róck:

blóod, but by my Fáther which ís in héa - ven.
I will búild my Chúrch.

Full
Al - le - lú - ia.

Offertory as at № 717 *(page 160)* Thou shalt make them.

Communion   Tone I

Cantors
Thóu art Pé - ter, and up - ón this róck:

Choir
I will búild my Chúrch.

729 THE HOLY NAME

Introit Tone VII

Cantors

In the Náme of Jésus let évery knée be bówed,

of things, abóve, and thíngs in éarth, and thíngs

Choir

be - néath: and let évery tóngue conféss and

acknówledge that Jésus Chríst is Lórd, to the

FINE

gló - ry of Gód the Fá - ther.

Cantors

Ps. O práise the Lórd, for the Lórd is grá - cious:
O Lórd, our gó-vern - or:

Choir

O sing práises únto his Náme, for it is lóve - ly.
how éxcellent is thy Náme in áll the wórld.

Cantors

Gló - ry be . . . and to the Hó - ly Ghóst.

Choir

As it wás . . . and év-er sháll be: wórld with-

Full

-óut énd. A - men. In the Náme of Jésus (*etc.*)

THE HOLY NAME (continued)

Gradual   Tone V

Cantors

God the Fáther hath sét Jésus Chríst at his ówn
De - lí - ver us, O Lórd our Gód, and gáther us

right hánd in the héavenly pláces; fár above all
from a-

principálity, and pówer, and míght, and do-mí - nion:
móng the héa - then:

Choir

and évery náme that is námed, not ónly in this
that wé may give thánks unto thy hóly Náme; and

world, but álso in thát which ís to cóme; and
máke our

háth put áll things ún - der his féet.
bóast of thy práise.

Cantors

℣. Hélp us, O Gód of óur sal -
℣. Thóu, O .Lórd, art our Fáther, and óur Re -

Choir

- vá - tion: and for the glóry of thy Náme,
-déem - er: thy Náme is from

O Lórd, deliver us; and be mérciful unto

our síns, for thy Náme's sáke.
év - er - lást - ing.

Alleluia   Tone VI

Cantors
Al - le - lú - ia. Al - le - lú - ia.

Cantors
℣. Swéet to the héart is the Náme of Jé-sus Chríst:
℣. *My móuth shall spéak the práise of   the   Lórd:*

Choir
músic to the éar;   hóney to the táste;
and lét all flésh give thánks un -

which túrns the héart to jóy and práise; and púts

to flíght the de - spíte of the wórld.
to   his   hó - ly   Náme.

Full
Al - le - lú - ia.

Offertory   Tone II

Cantors
In mý Náme shall they cást out dévils, they shall spéak
I will thánk thee, O Lórd   my   Gód,

Choir
with néw   tóngues: théy shall táke up sérpents; and
with áll my héart: and will práise thy

if they drínk any déadly thíng, it shall nót húrt them.
Náme for év - er - more.

Cantors
They shall láy hánds, O Lórd, up-ón   the síck.
For thóu, O Lórd, art góod and grá - cious:

THE HOLY NAME (continued)

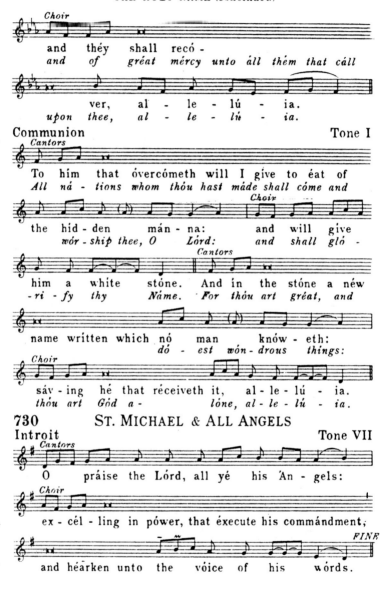

Choir

and   théy   shall   recó -
and   *of*   *gréat*   *mércy*   *unto*   *áll*   *thém*   *that*   *cáll*

ver,   al - le - lú - ia.
upon   *thee,*   *al - le - lú - ia.*

Communion   Tone I

Cantors

To   hím   that   óvercómeth   will   I   gíve   to   éat   of
All   *ná - tions*   *whom*   *thóu*   *hast*   *máde*   *shall*   *cóme*   *and*

Choir

the   híd - den   mán - na: and   will   gíve
wór - ship   *thee, O*   *Lórd:*   *and*   *shall*   *gló -*

Cantors

hím   a   white   stóne.   And   ín   the   stóne   a   néw
-ri - fy   *thy*   *Náme.*   *For*   *thóu*   *art*   *gréat, and*

name   wrítten   which   nó   man   knów - eth:
dó - est   *wón - drous*   *things:*

Choir

sáv - ing   hé   that   réceiveth   it,   al - le - lú - ia.
thóu   *art*   *Gód a -   lóne, al - le - lú - ia.*

730   ST. MICHAEL & ALL ANGELS

Introit   Tone VII

Cantors

O   práise   the   Lórd,   all   yé   his   'An - gels:

Choir

ex - cél - ling   in   pówer,   that   éxecute   his   commándment,

FINE

and   héarken   unto   the   vóice   of   his   wórds.

Cantors / Choir

Ps. Práise the Lórd, O my sóul: and áll that is withín me práise his hó - ly Náme.

Cantors

Gló - ry be . . . and to the Hó - ly Ghóst.

Choir

As it wás. . . .and év - er sháll be: wórld with- óut énd. A - men.

Full

O práise the Lórd *(etc.)*

Gradual Tone V

Cantors

O práise the Lórd, ye Ángels of his, yé that ex - cél in stréngth:

Choir

yé that ful - fil his com - mánd - ment.

Cantors

℣. O práise the Lórd, O my sóul: and áll that ís within

Choir

me práise his hó - ly Náme.

Alleluia Tone VI

Cantors / Choir

Al - le - lú - ia. Al - le - lú - ia.

ST. MICHAEL & ALL ANGELS (continued)

Cantors

℣. In the présence of the
℟. Hó - ly Míchael Archángel, defénd us in

'An - gels: will I práise
the dáy of bát - tle: *that we pérish nót*

Choir

thee, O Lórd my Gód.
in the dréad - ful júdge - ment.

Full

Al - le - lú - ia.

Offertory   **Tone II**

Cantors

An 'An - gel stóod by the áltar of the témple,

Choir

háving a gólden cén - ser in his hánd: and thére

was gíven unto him much íncense, and the smóke of the

íncense ascénded úp to Gód, al - le - lú - ia.

Communion   **Tone I**

Cantors

O ye 'Angels of the Lórd, bléss ye the

Choir

Lórd: síng ye práises, and mágnify

him a - bóve áll for év - er.

731 ALL SAINTS

Introit Tone VII

Re - jóice we áll, and práise the Lórd,

célebrating a hóly-dáy in hó - nour. of áll the

Choir

Sáints: in whóse solémnity the Ángels are jóyful,

FINE

and gló - ri - fy the Són of Gód.

Cantors

Ps. Re - jóice in the Lórd, O ye rígh - teous:

Choir

for it becómeth wéll the júst to be thánk - ful.

Cantors

Gló - ry be . . . and to the Hó - ly Ghóst.

Choir

As it wás . . . and év - er shall be: wórld with-

Full

-óut énd. A - men. Re - jóice we áll *(etc.)*

Gradual Tone V

Cantors

O féar the Lórd, all ye Sáints of his:

Choir

for théy that féar him lack nó - thing.

ALL SAINTS (continued)

℣. But they that seek the Lord: shall want no

manner of thing that is good.

Alleluia   Tone VI

Al - le - lú - ia.   Al - le - lú - ia.

℣. The saints shall judge the nations, and have dominion
℣. Come un - to mé, all yé that lábour and are héavy

over the peo - ple: and their Lord shall reign for ev - er.
lá - den; and   I will give you rést.

Al - le - lú - ia.

Offertory   Tone II

O God, won - derful art thou in thy holy pláces;
The souls of the righteous are in the hand of

even the God of Israel, he will give strength and power
God; and thére shall

un - to his peo - ple: blessed be
no tór-ment touch them: in the sight of the unwise they

God, al - le - lú - ia.
séemed to die, but they are in péace, al - le - lú - ia.

Communion   Tone I

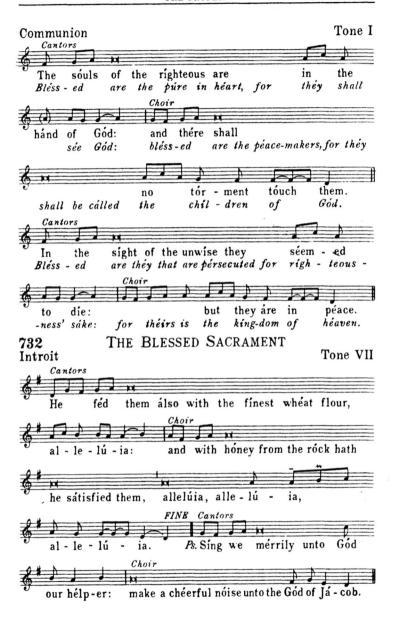

Cantors

The sóuls of the ríghteous are   in   the
Bléss - ed   are   the púre in héart, for   théy shall

Choir

hánd of Gód: and thére shall
sée Gód: bléss - ed   are the péace-makers, for théy

no   tór - ment tóuch them.
shall be cálled the   chíl - dren of   Gód.

Cantors

In   the   sight of the unwíse they   séem - ed
Bléss - ed   are théy that are pérsecuted for rígh - teous -

Choir

to   die: but   they áre in   péace.
-ness' sáke: for théirs is   the   king-dom of   héaven.

732   THE BLESSED SACRAMENT

Introit   Tone VII

Cantors

He   féd   them álso with the fínest whéat flour,

Choir

al - le - lú - ia: and with hóney from the róck hath

he sátisfied them,   allelúia, alle - lú - ia,

FINE Cantors

al - le - lú - ia.   Ps. Síng we mérrily unto Gód

Choir

our hélp-er: make a chéerful nóise unto the Gód of Já - cob.

THE BLESSED SACRAMENT (continued)

Cantors

Gló - ry be....... and to the Hó - ly Ghóst:

Choir

As it wás.... and év- er sháll be: wórld with-óut

Full

énd. A - men. He féd them álso *(etc.)*

Gradual   Tone V

Cantors

The éyes of áll wáit up - on thée, O Lórd:

Choir

and thou gívest them their méat in due séa - son.

Cantors   *Choir*

℣. Thou ó - pen - est thy hánd: and fíllest

áll things lív - ing with plén - teous - ness.

Alleluia   Tone VI

Cantors   *Choir*

Al - le - lú - ia. Al - le - lú - ia.

Cantors

℣. My Flésh is méat indéed, and my Blóod is drínk in - déed:

Choir

hé that éateth my Flésh and drínketh my Blóod,

dwélleth in mé, and I in hím.

Then at once, without any repetition of Alleluia, *is sung the following:*

Sequence   Modes VII & VIII

Láud, O Sí-on, thy sal-vá-tion, Láud with hýmns of
ex-ul-tá-tion Chríst, thy Kíng and Shép-herd trúe:

Spénd thy-self, his hó-nour ráis-ing, Who sur-páss-eth
áll thy práis-ing; Né-ver canst thou réach his dúe.

Síng to-dáy the mýs-tery shów-ing Of the lív-
-ing, lífe-be-stów-ing Bréad from héaven be-fóre thee sét;

É'en the sáme of óld pro-víd-ed, When the Twélve,
di-víne-ly gúid-ed, At the hó-ly Tá-ble mét.

Fúll and cléar ring óut thy chánt-ing, Jóy nor swéet-est
gráce be wánt-ing To thy héart and sóul to-dáy.

THE BLESSED SACRAMENT (continued)

Men

When we ga-ther up the mea-sure Of that Sup-per

and its trea-sure, Keep-ing feast in glad ar-ray.

Trebles

Lo, the new King's Ta-ble grac-ing, This new Pas-

-so-ver of bless-ing Hath ful-fill'd the eld-er rite;

Men

Now the new the old ef - fa - ceth, Truth re - veal'd

the sha-dow chas-eth, Day is break-ing on the night.

Trebles

What he did at Sup-per seat-ed, Christ or-dain'd to

be re - peat-ed, His me-mor-ial ne'er to cease:

Men

And, his word for guid-ance ta-king, Bread and wine we

hal - low, ma-king Thus our Sa - cri - fice of peace.

Trebles

This the truth to Chris-tians giv - en, Bread be - comes

his Flésh from héa-ven, Wíne be-cómes his hó - ly Blóod.

Men

Dóth it páss thy com-pre-hénd-ing? Yét by fáith, thy

síght tran-scénd-ing, Wón-drous thíngs are ún-der-stood.

Trebles

Yéa, be - néath these sígns are híd-den Gló - rious thíngs

to síght for-bíd-den; Lóok not on the óut-ward sígn.

Men

Wíne is póur'd and Bréad is bró-ken, But in éi - ther

sá - cred tó - ken Chríst is hére by pówer di - víne.

Trebles

Whó-so of this Fóod par-ták-eth, Rénd-eth not the

Lórd nor bréak-eth: Chríst is whóle to áll that táste.

Men

Thóu-sands are, as óne, re-céiv-ers Óne, as thóu-sands

of be-líev-ers, Tákes the Fóod that cán-not wáste.

THE BLESSED SACRAMENT (continued)

Trebles

Good and é-vil mén are shár-ing Óne re-pást, a

doom pre-pár-ing Vá-ried as the héart of mán;

Men

Dóom of life or déath a-wárd-ed, As their dáys

shall be re-córd-ed Whích from óne be-gin-ning rán.

Trebles

Whén the Sá-cra-ment is bró-ken, Dóubt not in each

sé-ver'd tó-ken, Hál-low'd by the wórd once spó-ken,

Men

Rést-eth áll the trúe con-tént. Nóught the pré-cious Gíft

di-ví-deth, Bréak-ing but the sígn be-tí-deth,

Hé him-sélf the sáme a-bí-deth, Nó-thing of his

Trebles

fúll-ness spént. Ló! the Án-gels' Fóod is gí-ven To

the píl-grim who hath strí-ven; Sée the chíl-dren's

Bréad from héa-ven, Whích to dógs may nót be cást;

Men

Trúth the án-cient týpes ful- fíll - ing, Í - saac bóund,

a víc-tim wíll-ing, Pás-chal lámb, its lífe-blood spíll-

Trebles

-ing, Mán-na sént in á - ges pást. Vé - ry Bréad,

good Shép-herd, ténd us, Jé-su, of thy lóve be-fríend us,

Thóu re-frésh us, thóu de-fénd us, Thíne e - tér - nal

góod-ness sénd us In the Lánd of lífe to sée;

Men

Thóu who áll things cánst and knów-est, Whó on éarth

such fóod be - stów-est, Gránt us with thy Sáints, though

lów-est, Whére the héav'n-ly Féast thou shów-est, Fél-low-

Full

héirs and guésts to be. A - men, Al-le-lú - ia.

THE BLESSED SACRAMENT (continued)

Offertory   Tone II

Cantors

The priests of the Lórd do óffer the ófferings of the Lórd, made by fíre and the bréad of their Gód:

Choir

thére-fore théy shall be hóly únto their Gód, and nót profáne the Náme of their Gód, al - le - lú - ia.

Communion   Tone I

Cantors

As óf-ten as ye do éat of this Bréad, and drínk this cúp:

Choir   *Cantors*

yé do shów the Lórd's déath till he cóme. Whére-fore, whósoever shall éat of this Bréad, and drínk of this Cúp of the Lórd un-wór-thi-ly:

Choir

shall be gúilty of the Bódy and Blóod of the Lórd, al - le - lú - ia.

733   THE DEPARTED

Introit   Tone VII

Cantors

Rest e - tér - nal gránt un - to thém, O Lórd:

Choir   *FINE*

and may líght per-pé-tu - al shíne up - ón them.

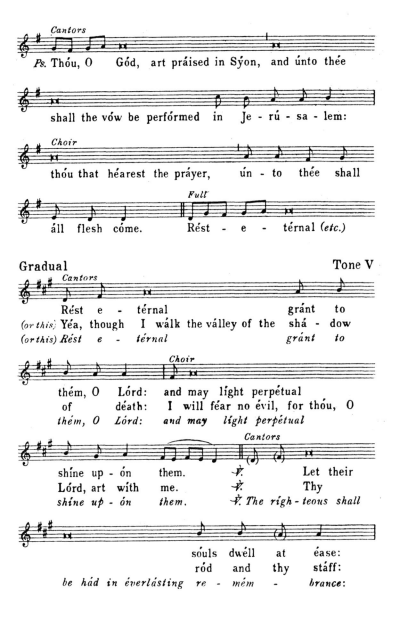

Ps. Thóu, O Gód, art práised in Sýon, and únto thée shall the vów be perfórmed in Je-rú-sa-lem:

Choir

thóu that héarest the práyer, ún-to thée shall áll flesh cóme. *Full* Rést-e-térnal (*etc.*)

Gradual

Tone V

Cantors

Rést e-térnal gránt to
(*or this*) Yéa, though I wálk the válley of the shá-dow
(*or this*) Rést e-térnal gránt to

Choir

thém, O Lórd: and may líght perpétual
of déath: I will féar no évil, for thóu, O
thém, O Lórd: and may líght perpétual

Cantors

shíne up-ón them. ℣. Let their
Lórd, art with me. ℣. Thy
shíne up-ón them. ℣. *The rígh-teous shall*

sóuls dwéll at éase:
ród and thy stáff:
be hád in éverlásting re-mém-brance:

THE DEPARTED (continued)

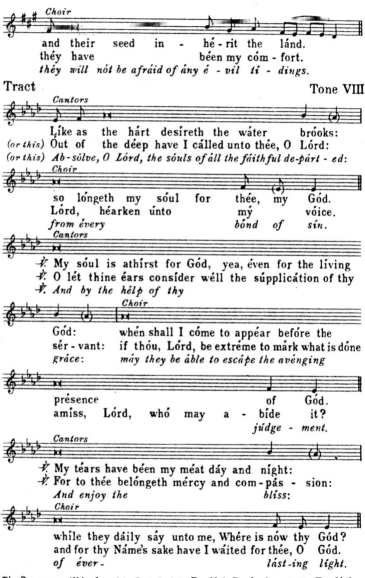

Choir

and their seed in - hé - rit the lánd.
théy have béen my cóm - fort.
théy will nót be afráid of ány é - vil tí - dings.

Tract   **Tone VIII**

Cantors

Líke as the hárt desíreth the wáter bróoks:
(*or this*) Out of the déep have I cálled unto thée, O Lórd:
(*or this*) *Ab-sólve, O Lórd, the sóuls of áll the fáithful de-párt - ed:*

Choir

so lóngeth my sóul for thée, my Gód.
Lórd, héarken únto mý vóice.
from évery bónd of sín.

Cantors

℣. My sóul is athírst for Gód, yea, éven for the líving
℣. O lét thine éars consíder wéll the súpplicátion of thy
℣. *And by the hélp of thy*

Choir

Gód: when shall I cóme to appéar befóre the
sér - vant: if thóu, Lórd, be extréme to márk what is dóne
gráce: *máy they be áble to escápe the avénging*

présence of Gód.
amíss, Lórd, whó may a - bíde it?
júdge - ment.

Cantors

℣. My téars have béen my méat dáy and. níght:
℣. For to thée belóngeth mércy and com-pás - sion:
And enjoy the blíss:

Choir

while they dáily sáy unto me, Whére is nów thy Gód?
and for thy Náme's sake have I wáited for thée, O Gód.
of éver - lást-ing líght.

The Sequence will be found in Part I of the English Gradual, *or in the* English Hymnal, *No. 351.*

Offertory   Tone II

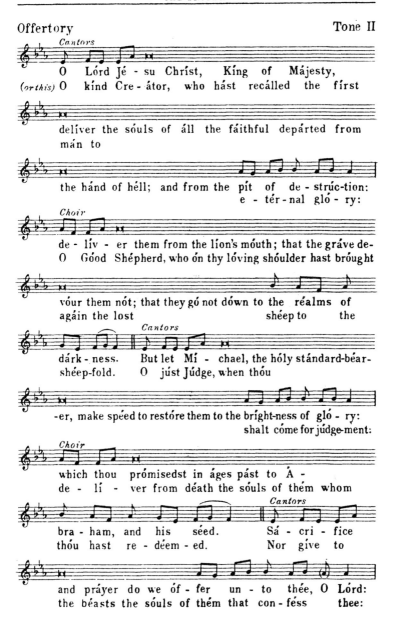

Cantors

O   Lórd Jé - su Chríst,   Kíng   of   Májesty,
(or this) O   kínd Cre - átor,   who hást recálled the   fírst

delíver the sóuls of áll the fáithful depárted from
mán to

the hánd of héll; and from the pít   of   de - strúc-tion:
           e - tér - nal gló - ry:

Choir

de - lív - er them from the líon's móuth; that the gráve de-
O   Góod   Shépherd, who ón thy lóving shóulder hast bróught

vóur them nót; that they gó not dówn to the   réalms   of
agáin the lost   shéep to   the

Cantors

dárk - ness.   But let Mí - chael, the hóly stándard-béar-
shéep-fold.   O   júst Júdge, when thóu

-er, make spéed to restóre them to the bríght-ness of gló - ry:
           shalt cóme for júdge-ment:

Choir

which thou   prómisedst in áges pást to À -
de - lí - ver from déath the sóuls of thém whom

Cantors

bra - ham, and   his   séed.   Sá - cri - fice
thóu hast re - déem - ed.   Nor gíve to

and práyer do we óf - fer   un - to   thée, O Lórd:
the béasts the sóuls of thém that con - féss   thee:

Choir

dó thou accépt them for the sóuls depárted, in whose
nor for - sáke them ut-

Cantors

mémory we máke this o - blá - tion.   And gránt them,
ter - ly for év - er.

Choir

Lórd, to páss from déath un-to lífe: which thou prómisedst

in áges pást unto Á - bra - ham   and   his   séed.

Communion   Tone I

Cantors

To thém in whose mémory the Bódy of
(*or this*) May líght etérnal shíne, O

Choir

Chríst is re - céiv - ed: gránt, O   Lórd,
Lórd, up - ón them: for énd - less áges with

rést ev - er - lást - ing.
thy bléssèd ónes, for thóu art grá - cious.

Cantors

℣. And may líght per - pé - tu - al:
℣. Rést e - térnal gránt to thém, O   Lórd:

Choir

shíne up - ón them.
and may líght perpétu - al shíne up - ón them.

Cantors

To thém in whose mémory the Blóod of Chríst is re - céiv-ed:
For énd - less áges with thy bléssèd ónes:

Choir

gránt, O   Lórd, rést ev - er - lást - ing.
for thóu art grá - cious.

APPENDIX

1- Of the Holy Spirit; 2-Of the Blessed Sacrament; 3-Of the Sacred Heart; 4- For the Reunion of Christendom; 5-For the Propagation of the Faith; 6-For Pilgrims and Travellers;   7- At a Marriage;   8- St. Joseph.

Introit   **Tone VII**

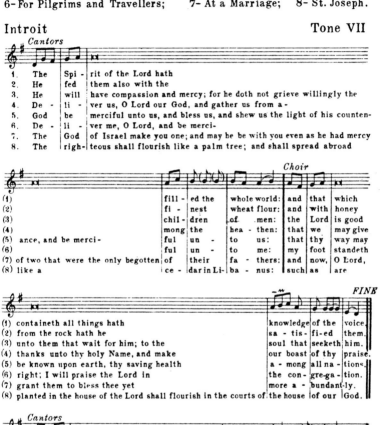

Cantors

1.	The	Spi - rit of the Lord hath
2.	He	fed them also with the
3.	He	will have compassion and mercy; for he doth not grieve willingly the
4.	De -	li - ver us, O Lord our God, and gather us from a-
5.	God	be merciful unto us, and bless us, and shew us the light of his counten-
6.	De -	li - ver me, O Lord, and be merci-
7.	The	God of Israel make you one; and may he be with you even as he had mercy
8.	The	righ- teous shall flourish like a palm tree; and shall spread abroad

Choir

(1)		fill - ed the	whole world:	and	that	which
(2)		fi - nest	wheat flour:	and	with	honey
(3)		chil - dren	of men:	the	Lord	is good
(4)		mong the	hea - then:	that	we	may give
(5)	ance, and be merci -	ful un -	to us:	that	thy	way may
(6)		ful un -	to me:	my	foot	standeth
(7)	of two that were the only begotten	of their	fa - thers:	and	now,	O Lord,
(8)	like a	ce - dar in Li-	ba - nus:	such	as	are

FINE

(1)	containeth all things hath	knowledge	of the	voice.
(2)	from the rock hath he	sa - tis -	fi-ed	them.
(3)	unto them that wait for him; to the	soul that	seeketh	him.
(4)	thanks unto thy holy Name, and make	our boast	of thy	praise.
(5)	be known upon earth, thy saving health	a - mong	all na -	tions.
(6)	right; I will praise the Lord in	the con-	grega -	tion.
(7)	grant them to bless thee yet	more a -	bundant-	ly.
(8)	planted in the house of the Lord shall flourish in the courts of the house	of our	God.

Cantors

(1)	*Ps.* Let God	arise, and let his ene-	mies be	scat - ter -	ed:
(2)	*Ps.* Sing we	merrily unto	God our	help -	er:
(3)	*Ps.* My song	shall be alway of the loving-	kind - ness	of the	Lord:
(4)	*Ps.* O give	thanks unto the Lord, for	he is	gra -	cious:
(5)	*Ps.* Let the	people	praise thee,	O	God:
(6)	*Ps.* Be thou	my judge, O Lord, for I have walked	in - no -	cent -	ly:
(7)	*Ps.* Blessed	are all	they that	fear the	Lord:
(8)	*Ps.* It is	a good thing to give thanks	un - to	the	Lord:

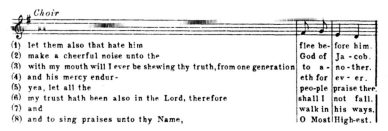

Choir

(1)	let them also that hate him	flee be-	fore him.
(2)	make a cheerful noise unto the	God of	Ja - cob.
(3)	with my mouth will I ever be shewing thy truth, from one generation	to a -	no - ther.
(4)	and his mercy endur-	eth for	ev - er.
(5)	yea, let all the	peo-ple	praise thee.
(6)	my trust hath been also in the Lord, therefore	shall I	not fall.
(7)	and	walk in	his ways.
(8)	and to sing praises unto thy Name,	O Most	High-est.

Glory be. As it was. *Repeat Introit.*

Gradual

Tone V

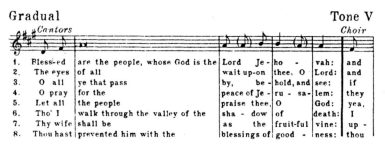

Cantors *Choir*

1.	Bless-ed	are the people, whose God is the	Lord	Je -	ho - vah:	and
2.	The eyes	of all	wait up-on	thee, O	Lord:	and
3.	O all	ye that pass	by,	be -	hold, and see:	if
4.	O pray	for the	peace of Je	ru - sa-	lem:	they
5.	Let all	the people	praise thee, O		God:	yea,
6.	Tho' I	walk through the valley of the	sha - dow	of	death:	I
7.	Thy wife	shall be	as the	fruit-ful	vine:	up -
8.	Thou hast	prevented him with the	blessings of	good -	ness:	thou

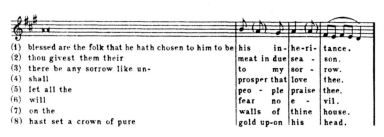

(1)	blessed are the folk that he hath chosen to him to be	his	in - he-ri-	tance.
(2)	thou givest them their	meat in due	sea -	son.
(3)	there be any sorrow like un-	to	my sor -	row.
(4)	shall	prosper that	love	thee.
(5)	let all the	peo - ple	praise	thee.
(6)	will	fear	no e -	vil.
(7)	on the	walls	of thine	house.
(8)	hast set a crown of pure	gold up-on	his	head.

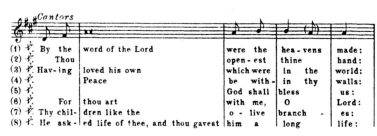

Cantors

(1) ℣.	By the	word of the Lord	were the	hea - vens made:
(2) ℣.	Thou		open - est	thine hand:
(3) ℣.	Hav-ing	loved his own	which were	in the world:
(4) ℣.		Peace	be with -	in thy walls:
(5) ℣.			God shall	bless us:
(6) ℣.	For	thou art	with me,	O Lord:
(7) ℣.	Thy chil-	dren like the	o - live	branch - es:
(8) ℣.	He ask-	ed life of thee, and thou gavest	him a	long life:

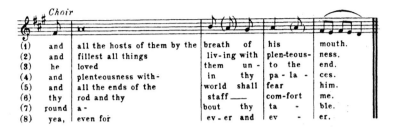

(1)	and	all the hosts of them by the	breath	of	his	mouth.
(2)	and	fillest all things	liv-ing	with	plen-teous-	ness.
(3)	he	loved	them	un -	to the	end.
(4)	and	plenteousness with-	in	thy	pa - la -	ces.
(5)	and	all the ends of the	world	shall	fear	him.
(6)	thy	rod and thy	staff ___		com-fort	me.
(7)	round	a -	bout	thy	ta -	ble.
(8)	yea,	even for	ev - er	and	ev -	er.

Alleluia

Tone VI

Al - le - lu - ia. Al - le - lu - ia.

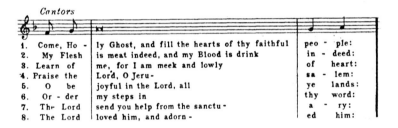

1.	Come, Ho -	ly Ghost, and fill the hearts of thy faithful	peo -	ple:
2.	My Flesh	is meat indeed, and my Blood is drink	in -	deed:
3.	Learn of	me, for I am meek and lowly	of	heart:
4.	Praise the	Lord, O Jeru-	sa -	lem:
5.	O be	joyful in the Lord, all	ye	lands:
6.	Or - der	my steps in	thy	word:
7.	The Lord	send you help from the sanctu-	a -	ry:
8.	The Lord	loved him, and adorn -	ed	him:

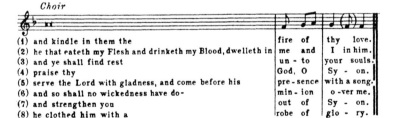

(1)	and kindle in them the	fire of	thy love.
(2)	he that eateth my Flesh and drinketh my Blood, dwelleth in	me and	I in him.
(3)	and ye shall find rest	un - to	your souls.
(4)	praise thy	God, O	Sy - on.
(5)	serve the Lord with gladness, and come before his	pre - sence	with a song.
(6)	and so shall no wickedness have do-	min - ion	o -ver me.
(7)	and strengthen you	out of	Sy - on.
(8)	he clothed him with a	robe of	glo - ry.

Full

Al - le - lu - ia.

Between Septuagesima and Easter, instead of Alleluia, *is sung the following:*

Tract   Tone VIII

Cantors

1.	O send	forth thy Spirit, and they shall be	made:
2.	From the	rising up of the sun, unto the going down of the	same:
3.	But I	am a worm, and no	man:
4.	In Jew -	ry is God	known:
5.	De - clare	the honour of the Lord unto the	hea - then:
6.	He shall	give his Angels charge over	thee:
7.	Lo, thus	shall the man be	bless - ed:
8.	Bless - ed	is the man that feareth the	Lord:

(1)	and thou shalt renew the face	of the	earth.
(2)	my Name shall be great among the	Gen -	tiles.
(3)	a very scorn of men, and the outcast of the	peo -	ple.
(4)	his Name is great in	Is - ra -	el.
(5)	and his wonders unto all	peo -	ple.
(6)	to keep thee in	all thy	ways.
(7)	that feareth	the	Lord.
(8)	he hath great delight in his com -	mand -	ments.

Choir

(1) ℣.	O how good and sweet, O	Lord:	
(2) ℣.	And in every place incense shall be offered unto my	Name:	
(3) ℣.	All they that see me laugh me to	scorn:	
(4) ℣.	At Salem in his taber -	na -	cle:
(5) ℣.	For the Lord is great, and cannot worthily be	prais -	ed:
(6) ℣.	They shall bear thee in their	hands:	
(7) ℣.	The Lord from out of Syon shall so bless	thee:	
(8) ℣.	His seed shall be mighty upon	earth:	

(1)	is thy Spirit with -	in	us.
(2)	and a pure	of - fer -	ing.
(3)	they shoot out their lips, and	shake their	heads.
(4)	and his dwelling in	Sy -	on.
(5)	he is more to be feared than	all	gods.
(6)	that thou hurt not thy foot a -	gainst a	stone.
(7)	that thou shalt see Jerusalem in pros -	pe - ri -	ty.
(8)	the generations of the faithful shall be	bless -	ed.

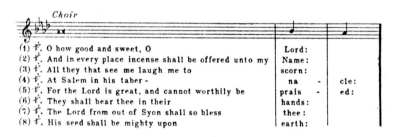

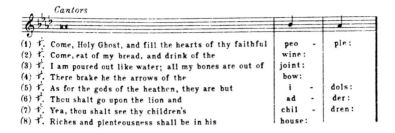

(1) ℣. Come, Holy Ghost, and fill the hearts of thy faithful	peo -	ple:
(2) ℣. Come, eat of my bread, and drink of the	wine:	
(3) ℣. I am poured out like water; all my bones are out of	joint:	
(4) ℣. There brake he the arrows of the	bow:	
(5) ℣. As for the gods of the heathen, they are but	i -	dols:
(6) ℣. Thou shalt go upon the lion and	ad -	der:
(7) ℣. Yea, thou shalt see thy children's	chil -	dren:
(8) ℣. Riches and plenteousness shall be in his	house:	

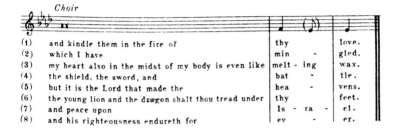

(1) and kindle them in the fire of	thy	love.
(2) which I have	min -	gled.
(3) my heart also in the midst of my body is even like	melt - ing	wax.
(4) the shield, the sword, and	bat -	tle.
(5) but it is the Lord that made the	hea -	vens.
(6) the young lion and the dragon shalt thou tread under	thy	feet.
(7) and peace upon	Is - ra -	el.
(8) and his righteousness endureth for	ev -	er.

During Easter-tide the foregoing Gradual *and* Alleluia *are omitted, and the following is sung:*

Alleluia   Tone VI

Al - le - lu - ia.   Al - le - lu - ia.

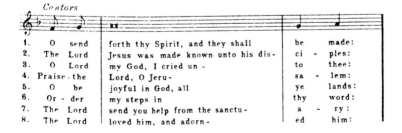

1.	O send	forth thy Spirit, and they shall	be	made:
2.	The Lord	Jesus was made known unto his dis-	ci -	ples:
3.	O Lord	my God, I cried un -	to	thee:
4.	Praise the	Lord, O Jeru-	sa -	lem:
5.	O be	joyful in God, all	ye	lands:
6.	Or - der	my steps in	thy	word:
7.	The Lord	send you help from the sanctu-	a -	ry:
8.	The Lord	loved him, and adorn-	ed	him:

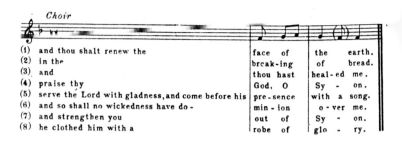

Choir

(1)	and thou shalt renew the	face of	the earth.
(2)	in the	break-ing	of bread.
(3)	and	thou hast	heal-ed me.
(4)	praise thy	God, O	Sy - on.
(5)	serve the Lord with gladness, and come before his	pre-sence	with a song.
(6)	and so shall no wickedness have do-	min-ion	o-ver me.
(7)	and strengthen you	out of	Sy - on.
(8)	he clothed him with a	robe of	glo - ry.

Full

Al - le - lu - ia.

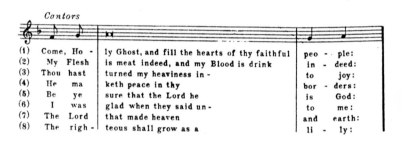

Cantors

(1)	Come, Ho -	ly Ghost, and fill the hearts of thy faithful	peo - ple:
(2)	My Flesh	is meat indeed, and my Blood is drink	in - deed:
(3)	Thou hast	turned my heaviness in -	to joy:
(4)	He ma	keth peace in thy	bor - ders:
(5)	Be ye	sure that the Lord he	is God:
(6)	I was	glad when they said un-	to me:
(7)	The Lord	that made heaven	and earth:
(8)	The righ -	teous shall grow as a	li - ly:

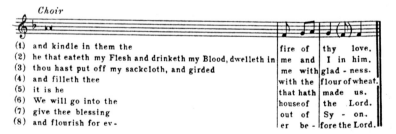

Choir

(1)	and kindle in them the	fire of	thy love.
(2)	he that eateth my Flesh and drinketh my Blood, dwelleth in	me and	I in him.
(3)	thou hast put off my sackcloth, and girded	me with	glad - ness.
(4)	and filleth thee	with the	flour of wheat.
(5)	it is he	that hath	made us.
(6)	We will go into the	house of	the Lord.
(7)	give thee blessing	out of	Sy - on.
(8)	and flourish for ev-	er be -	fore the Lord.

Full

Al - le - lu - ia.

Offertory

Tone II

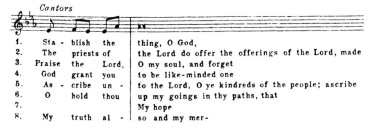

Cantors

1.	Sta - blish the	thing, O God,	
2.	The priests of	the Lord do offer the offerings of the Lord, made
3.	Praise the Lord,	O my soul, and forget
4.	God grant you	to be like-minded one
5.	As - cribe un -	to the Lord, O ye kindreds of the people; ascribe
6.	O hold thou	up my goings in thy paths, that
7.		My hope
8.	My truth al -	so and my mer-

(1)		that thou hast	wrought in us:
(2)	by fire, and	the bread of	their God:
(3)		not all his	be - ne - fits:
(4)		to - wards a -	no - ther:
(5)	unto the Lord	wor - ship and	pow - er:
(6)		my foot - steps	slip not:
(7)		hath been in	thee, O Lord:
(8)		cy shall be	with him:

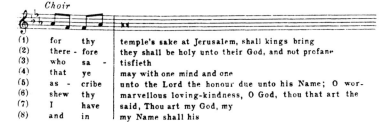

Choir

(1)	for thy	temple's sake at Jerusalem, shall kings bring
(2)	there - fore	they shall be holy unto their God, and not profane
(3)	who sa -	tisfieth
(4)	that ye	may with one mind and one
(5)	as - cribe	unto the Lord the honour due unto his Name; O wor-
(6)	shew thy	marvellous loving-kindness, O God, thou that art the
(7)	I have	said, Thou art my God, my
(8)	and in	my Name shall his

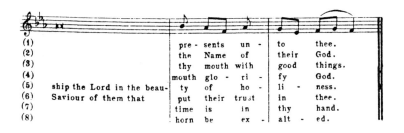

(1)		pre - sents un -	to thee.
(2)		the Name of	their God.
(3)		thy mouth with	good things.
(4)		mouth glo - ri -	fy God.
(5)	ship the Lord in the beau-	ty of ho -	li - ness.
(6)	Saviour of them that	put their trust	in thee.
(7)		time is in	thy hand.
(8)		horn be ex -	alt - ed.

Communion   Tone I

Cantors

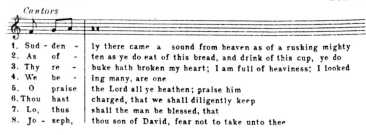

1. Sud - den - | ly there came a sound from heaven as of a rushing mighty
2. As of - | ten as ye do eat of this bread, and drink of this cup, ye do
3. Thy re - | buke hath broken my heart; I am full of heaviness; I looked
4. We be - | ing many, are one
5. O praise | the Lord all ye heathen; praise him
6. Thou hast | charged, that we shall keep diligently keep
7. Lo, thus | shall the man be blessed, that
8. Jo - seph, | thou son of David, fear not to take unto thee

(1) wind; and it filled all the house where | they were | sit - ting:
(2) shew the Lord's | death till | he come:
(3) for some to have | pi - ty | on me:
(4) | bread and one | bo - dy:
(5) | all ye | na - tions:
(6) | thy com - | mand - ments:
(7) | fear - eth | the Lord:
(8) | Ma - ry | thy wife:

Choir

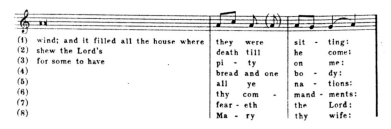

(1) and they | were all filled with the Holy Ghost; and began to speak the won-
(2) where-fore | whosoever shall eat of this bread, and drink of this cup of the Lord
(3) but there | was no man; neither found I a-
(4) for we | are all partakers of that
(5) for his | merciful kindness is even more and more towards us; and the
(6) O that | my ways were made so direct that I
(7) yea, that | thou shalt see thy children's children, and peace
(8) for that | which is conceived in her is

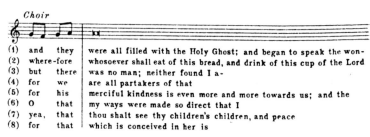

(1) | der - ful works | of God.
(2) unworthily, shall be guilty of the Body | and Blood of | the Lord.
(3) | ny to com - | fort me.
(4) | one bread and | one cup.
(5) truth of the Lord en- | dur - eth for | ev - er.
(6) | might keep thy | sta - tion.
(7) | up - on Is - | ra - el.
(8) | of the Ho - | ly Ghost.

IN TIME OF WAR

Introit – Call to remembrance *(page 47)*

Gradual – Thou art the God *(page 39)*

Alleluia – Deliver me from mine enemies *(page 118)*

Tract – O Lord, deal not with us *(page 42)*

Offertory – Thou shalt save the people *(page 116)*

Communion – Bow down thine ear *(page 114)*

FOR PEACE

Introit – Give peace, O Lord *(page 140)*

Gradual – O pray for the peace *(page 210)*

Alleluia – Praise the Lord *(page 211)*

Tract – In Jewry is God known *(page 212)*

Alleluia in Easter-tide – Praise the Lord *(page 213)*

Offertory – O praise the Lord *(page 54)*

Communion   Tone I

Peace I léave with you: my péace I gíve un-to you, sáith the Lord.

St. Gregory the Great

Introit – O ye priests of the Lord   *(page 168)*

Gradual   **Tone V**

The Lórd swáre, and will not re - pént:

Thóu art a príest for éver áfter the órder of Mel -

- chí - se - dech.   ℣ The Lórd said ún-to mý Lórd:

Sít thou on my ríght hánd.

Tract – Blessed is the man   *(page 166)*

Offertory – My truth also   *(page 167)*

Communion   **Tone I**

A fáith - ful and wíse stéward, whóm the Lórd set ó -

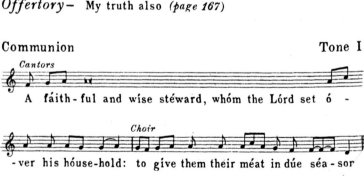

- ver his hóuse-hold: to gíve them théir méat in dúe séa - sor

OTHER FEASTS

Introit

Gradual

Tone V

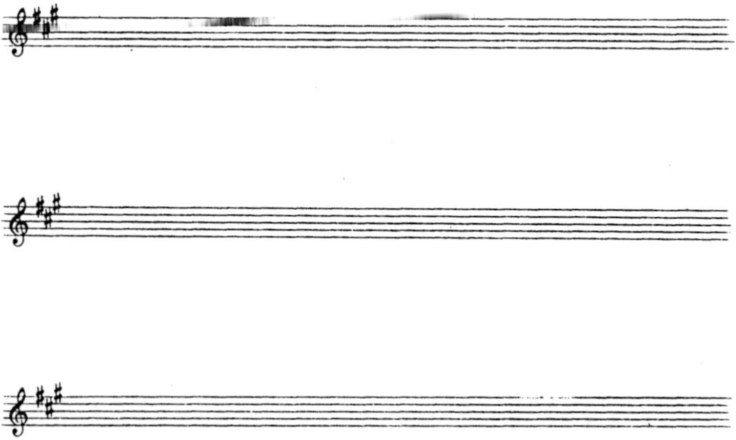

Alleluia

Tone VI

Cantors   *Choir*

Al - le - lú - ia.   Al - le - lú - ia.

Full

Al - le - lú - ia.

Offertory Tone II

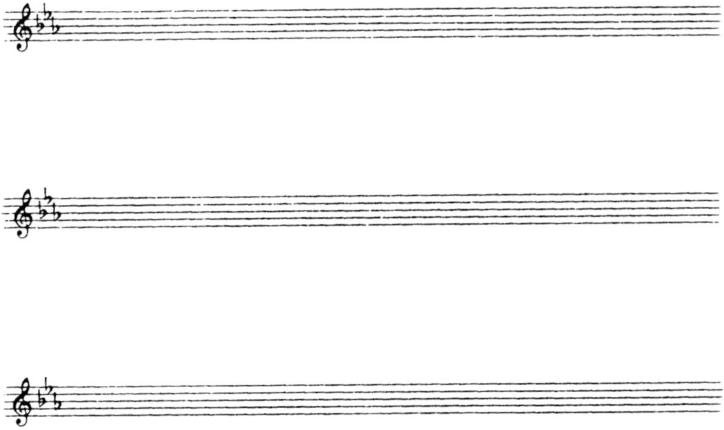

Communion Tone I

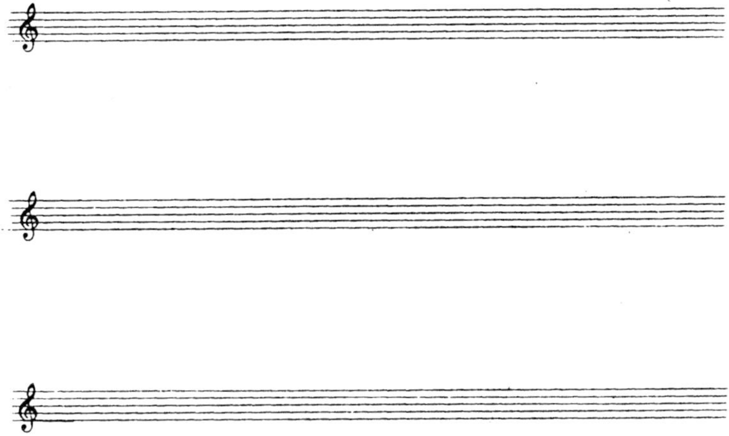

INDEX

DOMINE SALVUM FAC

The following Prayer for the King's Majesty is said at the conclusion of the principal Service on every Sunday in the year:

℣. O Lórd, sáve thy sérvant *Géorge,* our Kíng and Góvernor.

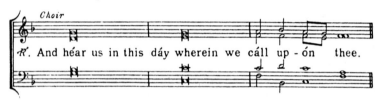

℟. And héar us in this dáy wherein we cáll up - ón thee.

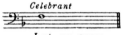

Let us pray.

Almighty God, whose kingdom is everlasting and power infinite; Have mercy upon the whole Church; and so rule the heart of thy chosen Servant *GEORGE,* our King and Governor, that he (knowing whose minister he is) may above all things seek thy honour and glory: and that we, and all his subjects (duly considering whose authority he hath) may faithfully serve, honour, and humbly obey him, in thee, and for thee, according to thy blessed Word and ordinance; through Jesus Christ our Lord, who with thee and the Holy Ghost liveth and reigneth, ever one God, world without end.

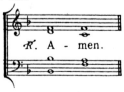

℟. A - men.

Lowe & Brydone Printers Ltd., London, N.W. 10.

Printed in the United States
102818LV00003B/28/A